Contents

Bullet Point One: The Second Reich

1. The Second Reich
2. World War One: Outbreak and Impact

Bullet Point Two: The Weimar Republic

3. The Weimar Republic 1919-23: Formation and problems
4. The Weimar Republic 1924-29: Stresemann Years

Bullet Point Three: Rise of the Nazis

5. The Development of the Nazi Party, 1920-29
6. The Rise of the Nazi Party, 1929-33

Controversy – Nazi Regime 1933-9

1. Core content
2. Efficiency
3. Popularity

Bullet Point Four: Wartime Germany

7. Life in Wartime Germany 1939-45

1. Past paper exam questions
2. Exam technique

1. The Second Reich

a) Social and economic changes
b) The political system of the Second Reich
c) Social divisions in the Second Reich
d) Elite versus working class politics in the Second Reich
e) The chancellorships of Von-Bulow and Bethmann-Hollweg
f) The constitution and distribution of political power

a) Social and economic changes

i) The Foundations of the Second Reich

c. 800, the geographical mass to become Germany was the Holy Roman Empire – it consisted of different kingdoms ruled by different groups; a loose affiliation of separate states rather than a unified country.

c. 1850, the North German Confederation of 22 independent states formed with 30 million inhabitants – this was the first modern German state, and predominantly controlled by Prussia.

In 1871, Germany was unified at the Hall of Mirrors, Versailles with the French royalty after the Franco-Prussian War. While a federated organisation of states had de facto existed earlier. Some states were joined forcibly through military power by Prussia, and each retained a local government, most with a royal family, controlling education, police and taxation. This collection of idiosyncratic states challenged national social unity.

ii) The Industrial Revolution

German industrialisation occurred with much greater rapidity, and later, than that of Britain. With this massive change brought huge urbanisation, and consequently a surge of working class politics combined with a new social and technological infrastructure.

1. Economic development (GDP)

1873	27bn marks
1894	45bn marks
1913	100bn marks

Index of industrial production: 21 (1871) to 100 (1913)

2. Social consequences

- 1871: 5% of population in cities; 1910: rises to 21%
- 1871: life expectancy 27; 1910: rises to 47

    - 1890-1914: 1% increase in real wages
    - 1900-1913: cost of living rise by 1/3

- Generally poor living conditions; homelessness grew, as did disease
    - Berlin Homeless Shelter Association accommodated 200,000 men a year after 1900
    - 1892- ten week cholera outbreak kills 8600 people

- But should not be exaggerated: in 1910, 1/5 Germans lived in large cities of over 100,000 but over 2/5 lived in small communities of less than 2000.

3. Social impact on groups in German society (in brief)

- The Working Classes
    - Strengthened working class identity
    - Rise of trade unions and grassroots pressure groups within SPD
    - The politicisation of workers; declining illiteracy – consequent rise of the SPD domination of Reichstag

- The Junkers
    - Relative decline of agriculture leads to pressures economically; labourers move to cities and industrialists challenge Junkers' political dominance
    - Policy of protectionism introduced in response to improved refridgeration and transportation; tariffs introduced for meat from USA (negative effect on industrialists).
    - Agrarian League formed in 1893; production exceeded demand so foreign export is subsidised. By 1907, 22% of global sugar beat market.

- The Mittelstand
    - Lower middle classes struggle to retain identity; fear of proletariatisation
    - Small businesses large part of economy: those with 1000 or more employees only 5% of workforce
    - Lack of social mobility due to Junker resistance to change

Germany was a class society to all extremes. This provides a context to the political phenomenon of both right-wing conservative political life and the rise of working class politics. However, before understanding these political developments, it is important to understand the political structure

b) The political system of the Second Reich

i) National political structure

Kaiser

- Authoritarian
- Divine right to rule
- Appoint/dismiss Chancellor
- Power over military and foreign policy
- King of Prussia
- Dissolve Reichstag at will
- Guardian of the Constitution

Chancellor & government ministers	Bundesrat	Reichstag
• Responsible / accountable to Kaiser only • Set government policy • Minister-President of Prussia • Aim to negotiate legislation through the Reichstag	• Represents 25 states • Approves all legislation • Power to change the constitution • Veto legislation with 14+ of 58 members' support; Prussia had 17 seats	• Elected by men over 25 • Could only dismiss / approve legislation put by Chancellor / Bundesrat • Most significant power control of defence and general budget

The military also swore an oath to the Kaiser, who was Commander in Chief. Its officers were from the Prussian aristocracy, and the respect of the army was so great that in some cases it could act almost unilaterally as a separate axis of government.

The distribution of political power and the extent to which this political system was one of parliamentary democracy will be considered later.

2. Federal political structure

While the national political structure was concerned with affairs of Germany's entire entity, such as war, foreign and economic affairs, the state-level political governances had power in education, health and local justice. Not only did states elect to the Bundesrat, but technically the princes of states held sovereignty over the Reich.

c) Social divisions in the Second Reich

i) Regional divisions

- Prussia was the land of the politically powerful, economic bourgeoisie and social elites

- Cities such as Berlin were rapidly urbanising and industrialising, with crowded housing and migration form the countryside

- Far-flung rural areas such as southern Bavaria did not see the fruits of industrialisation and lived in old wooden houses, relying on candlelight and water from the well living on estates owned by Junkers

ii) Ethnic divisions

- With Lithuanians and Poles in the East, Alsatians in the West, Nationalists and the Prussian government were preoccupied with the Poles and cooperated in campaigns for 'Germanisation'

iii) Class divisions

- As detailed above, the
    - Working classes
        - Industrialisation strengthened identity; rise of trade unions and class-consciousness / politicisation.
        - 3m votes for SPD in 1903, and 110/397 Reichstag seats 1912

    - Middle classes
        - Lower middle classes fear of proletariatisation
        - Upper middle restricted social mobility

- Not a homogenous identity; upper level of professions and civil servants, with lower level white collar workers self employed artisans and traders

- Junker classes
    - Protectionism of agriculture; began to pursue tariffs which hurt industrialists' exports where other countries followed with tariffs on German goods
    - Interested in preserving wealth at the expense of the middle classes and working classes

iv) Religious divisions

- Southern Catholics and the Catholic Centre Party resisted the Northern Protestant states' centralising tendencies (e.g. May Laws of 1873-5 brought education to state control), and would largely side with conservatives however would sometimes align with the SPD.

- Bismarck feared loyalty to Rome would conflict with loyalty to the Empire

This fundamentally led to the extrapolation of tensions between:

- Left vs right
- Workers (proletariat) vs owners (bourgeoisie)
- Communists vs imperialists
- Urban vs rural

d) Elite vs working class politics in the Second Reich

Political representation for the elites and working classes was imperative for both groups; the nature of the political system determined the extent to which either group would or could be successful, with historiographical interpretations ranging from that of personal Kaiser rule (Rohl) to a structuralist interpretation of social forces determining constraints and abilities for the Kaiser (Wehler).

i) Elite politics in the Second Reich

The elites were the:

- Political elites *(Kaiser, Chancellor, ministers)*
- Army officers
- Junkers *(agricultural land owners)*
- Industrialists *(factory and big business owners)*

Kaiser

- Divine right to rule
- "Nothing should occur on this earth without having first heard [the Kaiser]" – Wilhelm II
- Could appoint the Chancellor, dissolve the Reichstag and had much effective control over German affairs, especially foreign policy
- Was of a wealthy, aristocratic Prussian family

The army

- The Kaiser was the Commander in Chief – the army swore an oath to the Kaiser rather than to the state
- The Kaiser appointed a Military Cabinet made up of military figures, which advised and chose the General Staff who organised all military affairs
- Its elite regiments and officers were aristocratic Prussian landowners
- The army could, if it willed, act unilaterally – it lay outside of the formal constitution, and had the right to declare martial law (army rule)

Junkers and industrialists

- The aristocratic landowning classes typically of Prussia, with those of 'new money' owning industrious factories were represented among several pressure groups and political parties (those in the Reichstag were unpaid)

    o The DKP - German Conservative Party (Junkers)
    o The FKP – Free Conservative Party (industrialists)
    o The NLP – National Liberal Party (bankers and industrialists)

Conservative groups in the Reichstag:

Year	Seats	% Reichstag
1887	220	48
1912	102	26

- Sammsungpolitik, the politics of concentration, was an alliance of conservative interests through conservatives, liberals, Junkers and industrialists for a broad front against socialism.

- Economic pressure groups

    o Agrarian League

    Founded by Junkers 1893, seeking protectionism and subsidisation of agriculture; nationalist and anti-Semitic; supported by peasants. Over 300,000 members by 1914, working closely to DKP

    o Central Association of German Industrialists

    At the 1912 election, funded 120 candidates at the cost of 1m marks – the most popular pressure group by a considerable margin.

- Foreign policy pressure groups

    o German colonial league (pro-colonisation)
    o Pan Germany League (pro-colonisation and Germanisation)
    o Navy League (demanded Naval expansion; 1m members 1914)

Weltpolitik und Flottenpolitik united conservative groups in Sammsungspolitik

ii) Working class politics in the Second Reich

With economic growth and industrialisation, working class politics grew significantly in this period and evoked responses from the elite in power:

The SPD and organisation

- The SPD was founded in 1890, as a de facto re-founding of the SAPD (from 1875) having been unbanned. It consisted of two significant groups:

    o Reformers – non Marxist socialists working within the system
    o Revolutionaries – Marxist socialists favouring proletariat revolution; Ferdinand Bebel and Wilhelm Liebknecht involved in 1848, before exile in London and after helping to lead the Party from the 1870s

- Working class culture developed, with grassroots organisation. The SPD became increasingly powerful and gained more support

Elite responses to working class politics

- First response: Ban it! (Bismarck)

    o From 1878-90, anti-socialist laws were introduced where spreading socialist ideas became illegal under Bismarck. This affected working class organisations, with 45 newspapers shut down. The policy was justified by a radical assassination attempt on the Kaiser in 1878.

    o But this response fundamentally failed: the SPD got around it by publishing speeches in the Reichstag (uncensorable due to privilege); the tactic fundamentally backfired when the party returned as more Marxist and hardline, with 20% of the vote in 1890

- Second response: Unban it! (Caprivi [Chancellor 1890-4])

    o Allowed anti-socialist legislation to lapse, but brought in social reforms to undercut the appeal of the SPD. In 1891, Sunday and child labour was prohibited. However conservatives thought the Chancellor was himself a socialist, and he was removed rom his position. Nevertheless, he was successful in undermining the Marxist wing of the SPD.

- o With socialist organisations unbanned, there was much conflict between employees and workers during this time. Employers attempted to act paternally to support workers, for example buying housing where they would have to follow their rules. The Mansfield Strike of 1909 was a political strike where a company producing copper (the Mansfield Copper Mining Company) sacked 50 workers that participated in socialist agitation (recruiting for the SPD), which lasted 5 weeks before people had to return to work. Local military had supported the company, with troops preventing picketing during the strike.

- Third response: Construct an alternative

    - o Sammlungspolitik and Weltpolitik were devised as fashionable new alternatives: empire building through a Navy (Flottenpolitik) and imperialism, similar to Disraeli's approach of Tory democracy in Britain.

    - o Von Bulow (1900-9) having been Foreign Secretary from 1897, working with Von Tirpitz, satisfied everyone from the Kaiser to industrialists to hopefully the working classes. The Navy League was formed in 1898, with Naval laws passed in 1898, 1900, 1906, 1908, and 1912.

- But there was still conflict. The SPD and Liberal Party were agitated by tariffs that increased the price of bread under Prussian protectionism in 1902; this led to a surge of SPD support in the 1903 election. It also became clear that building a Navy and empire would be expensive, and would require raising taxes. In 1905, both indirect (VAT-style) and inheritance taxes were rejected by the conservative groups and the SPD & Centre Party respectively.

- Nevertheless, in 1912-3 things came to a head; the 1911 Second Moroccan Crisis attempted to break the alliance between GB and France by the Kaiser; GB sending warships to protect French made Germany more passionate about building a larger Navy and an inheritance tax was introduced, with SPD's majority in the Reichstag.

- Fourth response: War!

Fisher argues that the fourth response to socialism was World War One. By sending the working classes to war, they would regain their nationalism and the SPD would be silenced by patriotism, rallying behind the flag. Nevertheless, this too was a failure – the Russian Revolution of 1917, together with the loss of the war, would not be an effective response to working class politics.

e) The chancellorships of Von Bulow and Bethmann-Hollweg

The chancellorships of each of these leaders provides a fantastic insight into the distribution of political power in the Second Reich, especially with regards to the Kaiser's personal rule, the Reichstag's influence and the unilaterally-acting army.

- Bernhard <u>von Bulow</u> (1900-1909)
- Theobald von <u>Bethmann-Hollweg</u> (1909-1917)

i) The chancellorship of von Bulow (1900-9)

The Kaiser needed a strong, ruthless Chancellor – but also one who was diplomatic and persuasive, working effectively with the Reichstag, while forwarding policies of conservative interests. Bulow was an aristocratic Junker, adventuring in foreign policy and colonial expansion, and was the first Chancellor the Kaiser truly trusted. Bulow said, "with me, personal rule [of the Kaiser] – in the good sense – would really begin.

But Bulow was a slippery eel! He "managed" the Kaiser, while the Kaiser thought he was in control. For example, he demanded the appointment of his former deputy, Von Richthofen as state secretary for foreign affairs. He consolidated authority of the Prussian ministry, demanding "exclusive control over the publication of information relating to ministerial deliberations". Clark argues he initiated a press management scheme that created a mini-cult of personality around the Chancellor.

He attempted to rally patriotic forces to make personal rule a reality, by creating conservative blocs focused on foreign policy through Sammlungspolitik.

- 1890-1906 Conservative-National Liberal Alliance
- 1907-1909 The Blue-Black Bloc (Conservative, Liberal and Centre Party)

This encouraged Navy laws:

- 1898: First Navy Law based on 'risk theory'
- 1900: Second Navy Law for 38 battleships over 20 years – pleased industrialists
- 1906: Third Navy Law for 6 more battle cruisers

and in some ways soaked up the pressure and tensions in Germany, together with more progressive social welfare legislation:

- 1900: Accident insurance law extended to more worker occupations
- 1903: Sickness insurance law amended for more generous sick leave (26 weeks instead of 13)
- 1908: restrictions on child labour

But, in 1902, the New Tariff Law restored the higher duty on imported agricultural products. But, the SPD became more popular and had 81 seats in the 1903 election, from 56, while conservatives saw their vote decline.

SPD dominance thus didn't allow Von Bulow to increase tax for the Navy in 1905. Both indirect and inheritance taxes were rejected by the SPD and the conservatives, suggesting something of deadlock between interests in the Reichstag.

The Herero Uprising 1904

Jan 1904: Herero people, indigenous people of German South West Africa, revolted against German colonist rule. Governor Von Leutwein had been the official governor appointed by the government to look over the colony, however at the uprising the Kaiser sent Lieutenant-General von Trotha in as a response. The result was genocide.

The indigenous population before the rebellion had been 80,000, and afterwards (1911) it was 15,000. A policy of genocide, with concentration camps using slaves for German businesses and medical research, was installed, along with forced migration to the waterless Namib Desert.

Von Bulow was critical, calling the response "contrary to Christian and humanitarian principle", but the army ignored this widespread attitude in Germany. The episode revealed the power of the army and the Kaiser to will its own way, with the army lacking accountability to parliament.

The Hottentot Elections 1907

The government proposed to compensate settlers after the Herero Uprising, but the SPD and Centre Party were opposed to this policy. Bulow dissolved the Reichstag, and consequently formed a 'Bulow Bloc' of right-wing parties, which made many gains – this indicated both the attitude of the German electorate and the Chancellor's ability to rally support.

	Number of seats
Conservatives	60
Free Conservatives	24
National Liberals	54
Left Liberals	49

The Daily Telegraph Affair 1908

In October 1908, the British newspaper The Daily Telegraph published an interview with the Kaiser, where he said that the German people were not friends of England and that he was thus in the minority. This alienated the German people and the Reichstag; it was not the Kaiser's job to represent the German people, but the Reichstag's. Von Bulow decided to side with the Reichstag, and the Kaiser was forced to write a grovelling apology where he had to promise to "respect the terms of the Constitution".

In July 1909, however, the Kaiser got his own back when he asked Von Bulow to resign, ostentatiously over the budget. The Chancellor ultimately required the support of the Kaiser to sustain his role. Nevertheless, after the incident the Kaiser generally withdrew himself from domestic affairs.

ii) The chancellorship of Bethmann-Hollweg (1909-17)

After von Bulow's resignation, the Kaiser wanted someone he could trust and control. Since Bethmann-Hollweg was primarily experienced in civil service (with an eye to detail and procedure) and fairly straightforward, a novice in foreign policy, his appointment gave Wilhelm II the ability to use his own initiative in the areas that suited him. He had hunted on the Kaiser's family estates while younger.

However Bethmann-Hollweg would be especially dependant on the Kaiser since he was not popular with the Reichstag. While Wilhelm II's withdrawal from domestic affairs may have lubricated his ability to pass reforms, in actuality the polarisation of the Reichstag combined with an unwillingness to form 'blocs' meant passing real reform was difficult.

Attempted reform, and the 1912 Election

The Prussian Parliament, which sent representatives to the Bundesrat, was based on a three-tier system based on tax income that hugely skewed election results. For example, in 1908 the SPD received 23% of the vote but gained 7 seats, whereas the Conservative candidate received 16% of the vote yet gained 212 seats. The SPD continually petitioned against this system and its injustice.

In 1910, Bethmann-Hollweg attempted to make this system fairer, but failed upon hostility from conservatives. He tried to appease the SPD in 1911 with the Imperial Insurance Code for health insurance for old aged or ill workers.

In the 1912 election, the radical left had formed a coalition (in 1910); high food prices and the Chancellor's unwillingness to campaign on a nationalist agenda through a bloc saw the SPD victorious. They gained 67 new seats, bringing their total to 110 and making them the largest party in the Reichstag.

But the SPD would not form a coalition with other parties in the Reichstag, making the Chancellor's job of passing legislation even more difficult. He had to work to invoke support for the 1913 Army Bill by promising that funds would derive from a direct property tax; the SPD did not want to appear unpatriotic in rejecting the bill.

The Zabern Affair 1913

The Reich won Alsace-Lorraine in 1871, and it did not have the same autonomy as other German states – instead being run by an Imperial Governor. 10% of the province were native French speakers, and barely tolerated by the Germans there. In 1911, Bethmann-Hollweg had attempted to appease them by giving them their own flag, constitution and national anthem.

In 1913, an officer referred to some of them as "wackes", an insulting term, and this was picked up on by the local press. A German officer named von Forstner, who made the comment, ordered his troops to respond violently if attacked by the locals; demonstrated staged by the Zabern residents were suppressed 'robustly' by the army. Socialists in Germany were disgusted by the actions of the army, and mass demonstrations broke out in key industrial centres organised by the SPD.

The Kaiser sided with the military and insisted on utilising his position as Commander in Chief of the army to deal with what he saw was an internal military matter. All actions would be taken in secret. The SPD disagreed, and as Clark argues, saw the matter as a "test case for the primacy of law and civil authority".

Bethmann sided with the army and the military, and the Reichstag responded with a vote of no confidence (293-54). The Kaiser nevertheless stood by the Chancellor, ignoring calls for his resignation.

The Affair was deeply symbolic of the power divisions in the Third Reich, and the lack of ability for either the Chancellor or the Reichstag to control the ary.

War and resignation 1914-7

Bethmann was at odds with the military from 1915, with the policy of unrestricted submarine warfare, managing to keep it at bay until 1917 where the Kaiser submitted to pressure. He also struggled with the military dictatorship with his attempts to offer the Allies peace terms in 1916-7, this created bad relationships with the 'silent dictatorship'.

In the wake of the February Revolution, the SPD's demands for (especially Prussian) franchise reform found sympathy with Bethmann; in 1917 he was successful in making the Kaiser more accommodating for this, which prompted the resignation of the silent dictatorship. 3-OHL ordered that Bethmann resign, but the Kaiser held firm and Hindenburg and Ludendorff offered their resignations in July 1917, the Kaiser subsequently abdicating in November 1918.

f) The constitution and distribution of political power

Remember that in 1914 the dynamic of power changes with the start of WWI and the ascendancy of the 'silent dictatorship', but on the whole the Second Reich should be the focus – specifically between the Kaiser, Reichstag, Chancellor, military and pressure groups. While an outline of constitutional differences in power is important, it is worth consideration that in de facto terms the division of power is quite different. The evidence for all points is above, but below is an outline of the distribution of political power in the Second Reich.

	Powerful	Not powerful
Reichstag	<ul><li>Constitutional powers and method of election</li><li>Attempt to reform Prussian voting system</li><li>Imperial Insurance Code</li><li>Sickness Insurance Law</li><li>1912 election</li><li>1905 budget</li></ul>	<ul><li>Zabern Affair</li><li>Herero Uprising</li><li>Does not hold the government to account</li><li>Federalism undermines national legislature</li><li>Comparative power of other bodies</li></ul>
Kaiser	<ul><li>Constitutional foreign policy domination</li><li>Zabern Affair</li><li>Navy Laws passed</li><li>Von Bulow's resignation</li><li>Protectionist tariff laws for Prussian purposes</li></ul>	<ul><li>Daily Telegraph Affair</li><li>1912 election</li><li>Military undermine foreign policy role</li><li>SPD / Bismarck – 'state socialism', social reforms</li><li>3-OHL prominence</li></ul>
Chancellor	<ul><li>Significant constitutional powers</li><li>Hottentot election</li><li>Daily Telegraph Affair</li><li>Can be manipulative of Kaiser, e.g. von Bulow's aims</li></ul>	<ul><li>Had to retain the support of the Kaiser, e.g. Herero Uprising vs Daily Telegraph Affair – accountable only to him</li><li>Required support of Reichstag, e.g. 1912 laws</li></ul>
Military	<ul><li>Herero Uprising and Zabern Affair – act unilaterally through huge respect in German society</li><li>September Programme of 1914, and creating a Mitteleuropa</li><li>WWI initiated without full support of Kaiser</li><li>'Silent dictatorship'</li></ul>	<ul><li>Only acted unilaterally on military affairs; did not engage in social, economic or constitutional affairs</li><li>Allowed to act in such a way by the Kaiser?</li></ul>

Historiographical perspectives on distribution of power

- Rohl: personal rule of the Kaiser, the Chancellor was only the personal tool of the Kaiser – this is best evidenced through "the social and socialist policies, the gigantic fleet-building programme and the Prussian canal policy".

- Blackbourn: the Kaiser had indirect influence, rather than direct constitutional authority as the powerful symbolic figure who set the tone of public life with his "role of 'strong man'"

- Wehler: a permanent state of crisis behind its façade of high-handed leadership – a continual power struggle due to the nature of the constitution; this was the cause of the zig-zag determination of policy.

- Feuchtwanger: potential for autocracy not actualised by the Kaiser due to his own ignorance, inconsistency and lack of a coherent plan.

Parliamentary democracy

Whether Germany is a parliamentary democracy or not is fundamentally the same question of power, but with focus on whether:

- The government is accountable to the Reichstag
- Whether Parliament has primary legislative authority
- Whether Germany was democratic (people power) rather than autocratic

An exam question could also focus on:

- A military dictatorship?
- A constitutional monarchy?
- A semi-autocracy?
- Prussian domination?
- Elitism?
- or on the relative impact of working class politics

2. World War One

a) The Outbreak of World War One
b) Military progress of World War One
c) The Political and Social Impact of World War One
d) Germany in 1918-9; revolutions and Weimar

a) The Outbreak of World War One

Bethmann-Hollweg, when asked how the war began, responded: "if only I knew".

On June 28th 1914, the heir to the Austro-Hungarian throne Franz Ferdinand was assassinated by a group of Bosnian Serb assassins in Sarajevo. The political objective was to break off Austro-Hungary's south-Slav provinces to create a Greater Serbia.

Five weeks later, Europe broke out into its first world war.

i) "The Four Steps to WWI"

1. Austria declares war

Austria hated Serbia, and nationalism was the largest threat to its very existence. In early July, Austria-Hungary approached Germany and gained a blank cheque for its support no matter what. It then sent Serbia an ultimatum with ten demands that they did not expect Serbia to accept, giving them an excuse to invade. Serbia accepted the conditions but nevertheless Austria declared war on the 28th of July.

2. Russia mobilises

While most had supported the Austrians in June, they now seemed war-mad; they shelled the Serbian capital Belgrade. Russia did not want war, but Serbia called on it as an ally after the Tsar had failed to support Serbia in the 1908 Bosnian crisis. Nicholas II decided to mobilise his army; at first he tried to mobilise his army only against Austria-Hungary however was informed this was not possible, so called for a general mobilisation before sending a telegram to the Kaiser saying it was not against Germany.

3. Germany's response – the Schlieffen Plan

Since Russia had mobilised, now it was Germany's turn to put into action its plan for mobilisation. The plan said that if there was a war, Germany would fight both France and Russia; France was weak, and had been defeated in 10 weeks in 1870, while Russia was slow – estimating it would take Russia 6 weeks to mobilise its army. The intention was to take out France quickly, allowing Germany to transport its army back to Russia. France did not mobilise, and this was costing Germany time, so on 1 August 1914 the Kaiser gave the order to mobilise the army, and on 3 August invaded France – the next day France declared war on Germany.

4. Britain declares war

The British had tried to avoid war and hold negotiations between powers to no effect. On the 1st of August, Britain told Germany that it would stay neutral so long as Germany did not invade France; the Kaiser wanted to agree, but had lost control of his generals who said this wasn't possible. On the 2nd of August, an error of the Schlieffen Plan saw German forces travelling through Belgium to get to France – however, Belgium refused to allow this so the next day Germany invaded Belgium. Hence, Britain was obliged under the 1939 Treaty of Washington to help Belgium in the effect of an invasion. Bethmann-Hollweg asked, "For a scrap of paper, Great Britain is going to make war?"

ii) The Outbreak of War: Domestic Factors

The outbreak of war was allowed by and catalysed certain feelings domestically in the people of Germany. On the outbreak of war, the Kaiser declared to the Reichstag: "I have no knowledge of party or creed…. I know only Germans".

For the Junkers, industrialists and upper classes, war would allow for great nationalism and patriotism – the rallying of the German people behind the German nation and military in lieu of socialist organisations gaining prominence. Indeed, as the clouds of war loomed over even the socialists thought it necessary to rally behind the flag and show their patriotism. While there was a sense of the war being a quick and easy victory, this sense of nationalism overcame prior internal social divisions of class, religion, region, political representation et cetera.

Germany would rally around Bergfrieden (fortress spirit), and the SPD voted almost unanimously in favour of the war in 1914 in the spirit of patriotism. When Bethmann-Hollweg asked for war funding worth £265million, it found unanimous support in the Reichstag across all parties.

So was Germany blameless?

While the SPD may not have known about it, the secret September programme of 1914 saw Bethmann-Hollweg envisage the taking over of territory from France, setting up a German economic zone of "Mittel Europa" – invading France was prerequisite.

b) Military progress of World War One

Having been sold to the German people as a quick and easy war, the failure of Germany to achieve a quick victory in the autumn of 1914 can be seen as resulting in a lengthy war for which the country was militarily, strategically and economically unprepared for.

Autumn 1914: The breakdown of the Schlieffen Plan

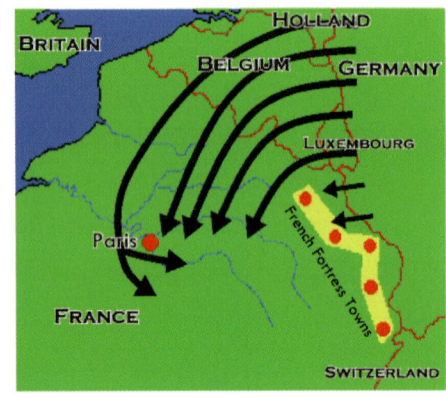

The Schlieffen Plan not provide any guarantee of success; indeed, plans changed before any shots were fired with the decision to avoid the Netherlands and change the route, together with the concern of a strong French assault in Alsace-Lorraine diverting troops to the south. Nevertheless, in August the Allies were in retreat and Germany's optimism in the plan and the war soared.

In September 1914, however, this optimism ebbed:

- Russia mobilised faster than expected, and in desperation Moltke (Chief of Supreme Army Command) transferred additional German units to the Eastern Front.
- Belgian resistance was stronger than expected
- The invasion of Belgium led to the British entering the war.

As German lines of communication lengthened, the speed of their advance slowed. In September, at the Battle of the Marne, the Germans were forced to retreat and the Plan had failed. Moltke suffered a nervous breakdown and resigned, and was replaced by Falkenhayn.

The war was at stalemate, with the Western Front having trenches dug for 400 miles. By November, Germany was confronted with a war on two fronts for which it was not prepared militarily. It had to develop an alternative strategy.

1915-6: The failure of alternative strategies

Germany failed to come up with an alternative strategy to military stalemate; victories on the Eastern Front against Russia and the withdrawal of Allies from the Dardanelles campaign could not alter the fact time was against Germany. The Allies gained maritime advantage through seizing German colonies, and destroying its roving cruisers that preyed on unarmed British merchant vessels. Indeed, Britain placed a naval blockade, which severely limited Germany's ability to import foodstuffs and raw materials for industrial militarisation.

Unrestricted submarine warfare

In 1915 Admiral Tirpitz pressed for the use of unrestricted submarine warfare and the sinking of all ships bound for Britain irrespective of their nationality in response to the British blockade. This led to fierce controversy, especially over its morality and would likely cause diplomatic issues with the then–neutral USA.

In February 1915, Bethmann-Hollweg took the military advice and the policy was introduced. However, after the sinking of the liner Lusitania in September and the loss of 1100 lives, the policy was dropped.

In February 1916, the policy was for a short time reintroduced but as the USA threatened to break off diplomatic relations, the policy was again dropped and Tirpitz resigned. More questions over how the war could be brought to a successful conclusion ensued.

Attrition (loss of troops)

Falkenhayn believed the war could only be won on the Western Front; his plan to launch a massive assault against the key French fortress town of Verdun was hence accepted. He declared his aim as to "bleed the French army white"; the casualties on both sides were horrifying, but the French held on and the losses at Verdun were added to those lost at the Battle of the Somme – fought later in 1916.

During the years 1915-6, the failure to make advances after the failure of the Schlieffen Plan saw the replacement of Falkenhayn in the summer of 1916 with Hindenburg and Ludendorff; as victory failed to militarise, economic consequences grew more intense.

1917: Submarine warfare and entry of the USA

Hindenburg and Ludendorff were both determined to pursue the war with vigour and the utmost nationalism and patriotism, yet did not offer a new military strategy. There was no way out of the Western Front deadlock, and the military again pressed for unrestricted submarine warfare in the belief this would bring Britain to its knees.

Bethmann was unconvinced of this miracle cure, but nevertheless, by January 1917 he was very unpopular and lacked political capital to meaningfully oppose the plan. In February, a new submarine warfare plan was launched.

The policy was a huge failure. Initially, Britain suffered terrible losses but the introduction of the convoy system where the Royal Navy countered the threat of submarines to merchant ships reduced the losses to tolerable levels. By 1918, it was clear the Germans were losing the submarine war. Moreover, the US decision to enter the war in April 1917 provided a major boost to the Alied campaign, and the military situation was stacked against Germany and the Central Powers (Austria-Hungary, Turkey, Bulgaria)

1918: The final German offensive

As 1917 drew to a close, Germany's defeat seemed only a matter of time – the fact that they did not surrender until November 1918 was mainly due to events in Russia; the revolution and the establishment of the Bolsheviks' regime in November 1917 resulted in Russia seeking an armistice with Germany by a negotiated peace in March 1918, the Treaty of Brest-Litovsk which held the following terms:

- o The previously Russian territories of Poland, Lithuania and Latvia annexed by Germany
- o Territories of Estonia and Ukraine became in effect German spheres of economic and military influence
- o Russia had to pay three billion roubles in reparations

These provisions boosted civilian and military morale; it also freed Germany from a two-front war and opened up the chance of victory through concentrating on the Western Front. Nevertheless, the Allied lines of defence were never decisively broken. One reason for this was poor strategy – for example, the German Supreme Command kept 1.5m men on the Eastern Front to maintain won territory, while those on the Western Front were met with increasing numbers of US troops.

Ludendorff Offensive

The Treaty of Brest-Litovsk, signed by the Russians in March 1918, did give 3-OHL the kindof annexation that they aspired to – handing over several regions. Germany furthermore seized three quarters of Russia's coal ad iron, virtually all oil and cotton, and a third of the Russian population. All parties in the Reichstag voted in favour except the USPD.

The attempt to seize the opportunity of this treaty was seen in the Ludendorff Offensive begun in March 1918. The country collectively held its breath as Germany focused on the Western Front, with half a million troops transferring. The aim was to deliver the Allies such a blow that they would withdraw from the war. Nevertheless, this was extremely optimistic given the Allies had 7m more military personnel and 47,000 more machine guns. On 21 March, the first German attack pushed Allied forces back considerable distances; by July they had pushed 80 miles and were spent – by September the Allies' counter-attack had pushed the Germans back to the Hindenburg Line.

German morale was significantly dented, and the 8th of August, where the German army was pushed back at Amiens by the British as the 'blackest day of the German army'

September to November 1918: Defeat, and armistice

By mid-September the final German defensive positions had been broken and the western region of Germany faced the very real possibility of invasion. In southeastern Europe, Germany's allies all faced imminent collapse.

Even Hindenberg and Ludendorff at last recognised the extent of the crisis and on 29 September they advised the Kaiser that Germany must make enquiries to request an armistice.

On October 4th, Germany's request for an armistice was refused. On October 29th, Germany's navy mutinied and by November 9th, the Kaiser abdicated the throne and two days afterwards Germany signed an armistice with the Allies officially ending WWI.

The reasons for Germany's failure in World War One can be summarised as follows:

- The failure of the Schlieffen Plan to achieve rapid victory in 1914
- Stalemate of a two-front war and trench warfare
- The failure of unrestricted submarine warfare
- Strength of the allies as major military and naval powers
- Limitations of the Imperial German war economy
- The failure to seize the opportunity of Brest-Litovsk in 1918

c) The Political and Social Impact of WWI

There are several major impacts of WWI on Germany, that led to the creation of the Weimar Constitution and two revolutions: one from above, and one from below. And this was before the Treaty of Versailles.

Political impact in Germany

- The emergence of the 'Silent Dictatorship'

The 3-OHL (Supreme Army Command) military dictatorship of Ludendorff and Hidenberg ascended through the considerably increasing power of the Supreme Command during the war, with the army deeply respected in German society. By means of threatening resignation, the Supreme Command could exert influence over political, social and military affairs. Indeed, after conservatives lamed Bethmann for abandoning unrestricted submarine warfare, Falkenhayn was ousted and the more popular leaders appointed as leaders of the Supreme Command in August 1916.

With massive popularity compared to Bethmann-Hollweg or the Kaiser, they established this control with relative ease. Nevertheless, they were unpopular with the urban working classes and the SPD. This was primarily due to their imperialist, traditional and autocratic aims synonymous with that of backwards, Imperial Germany:

- Pursuit of an annexationist peace
- Opposed domestic and social reform
- Façade of constitutionalism (Reichstag side-lined)
- Militarism – a very harsh Russian peace; unrestricted submarine warfare

This fundamentally produced a militarisation of German society, through policies such as the Auxiliary Service Law (in December 1916, which mobilised all available male labour for the war effort) and rejecting several opportunities for a negotiated peace.

- 1917 July Crisis

The leaders of the SPD continued to support the war, but only tentatively; they were the majority in the Reichstag, and the entry of America together, with the ending of Russian autocracy and the continuing failures of the German military made it increasingly difficult to support the war. The Kaiser was persuaded by Bethmann-Hollweg to give hope of reform and on 7 April 1917 gave his Easter address. The Kaiser promised in fairly vague terms an end to Prussia's three-tier voting system and to reform the Bundesrat when the war ended.

This did little, however, to appease people outside of the Reichstag that aimed for a peace without victory rather than a victorious peace. Indeed, in the debate on war credits at the start of July 1917, the SPD and Centre Party coalition tried to search for a 'peace without victory'; Bethmann-Hollweg, not sharing this view, lost the confidence of both the military command and the Reichstag and was forced to resign. He was replaced by a Ludendorff nominee, George Michaelis – strengthening the power of the silent dictatorship.

On the 19th of July, a majority in the Reichstag (212-116) voted in favour of a 'peace resolution' that promoted the idea of peace without annexation of land; this marked significant political polarisation in alignment with the social impact of the war (discussed below).

- o Political polarisation: opposition to the war

The Left

Growing opposition was found on the Home Front, in part due to the huge losses suffered; from 1914 to 1918, 13.2m were mobilised – there were 6.2m casualties and 2m were killed. Very few German villages and families remained untouched by the carnage. Many began to question the sacrifice – In May and June 1916, strikers in Berlin took to streets demanding "Freedom, Bread and Peace"; this was made worse by the extra economic strain of the Hindenburg Programme and the Auxiliary Service Law. Indeed, the Russian Revolution in Petrograd in March 1917 acted as an inspiration for the discontented, just as the American entry to the war revitalised the demand for change.

The announcement of a reduction in the bread ration in April 1917 was the catalyst for widespread strikes. In Berlin, over 300,000 workers demonstrated for food and an end to the war. Workers formed workers councils named Soviets in solidarity with Russian comrades. While the SPD did not support this, the workers too were alienated by the party that had thrown out its own members in March 1917 for refusing to vote in favour of war credits. Consequently, the party of Independent Socialists (USPD) was formed. By 1918, it has 100,000 members across Germany, calling for an immediate end to the war and a series of social reforms.

The Right

The Fatherland Party was founded in response to the Reichstag's 1917 Peace Resolution; the 'reconsolidation of the peoples' and peace without victory was incompatible with the aims of military acquisition of territory and imperialism. Admiral Tirpitz, of the policy of unrestricted submarine warfare, was the Chairman. The group quickly boasted 1.25m members by spring 1917, and was not just Junkers or Prussians. It professed the war could only be won through commitment and aimed to establish a military dictatorship.

The Right continued to campaign for annexationist Siegfrieden (victorious peace), inextricably combined with domestic political objectives of Junker hegemony, synonymous with the pre-war era.

Failed reconciliation of ideologies

- In August 1917, Richard von Kuhlman became German foreign secretary; he aimed to bring a negotiated peace without annexation but to extend German influence to the east; his moderation was too much for 3-OHL who engineered his dismissal in July 1918.

- In October 1917, Michaelis was sacked as the Reichstag passed a resolution supporting reform of the Prussian voting system.

- He was replaced by Count Hertling of the Centre Party who made conciliatory attempts of constitutional reform; the Prussian Parliament continued to debate reform but the conservatives ultimately made their opposition clear.

Social and economic impact

- Food

After Germany's submarine blockade on Great Britain in 1915, the British government responded by ordering the Royal Navy to seize all goods presumed to be destined for Germany – since Germany was not self-sufficient for food before the war (in 1914 importing 25% of what it consumed), this had a considerable impact. The state consequently assumed control of the food supply.

The Imperial Grain Corporation was established in 1915, and administered the rationing and distribution of grain; however through war-profiteering, 40 other Corporations were created which competed with the federal, state and regional governments to administer food supply. In order to bring some cohesion to this, the War Food Office was established in 1916 but without the power to exert control over other organisations; the bureaucratic jungle precipitated counter-productive decisions such as the slaughtering of 9m pigs that ate grain, limiting the supply of pork and fertilizer. Indeed, the German grain harvest decreased from 27m tonnes in 1914 to just 14.6m in 1917.

- Shortages

The impact of the blockage was similar to the problem of a shortage of labour in the countryside. By the end of 1914, around half of the agricultural workforce had been called up to serve. The conservatism of Germany meant that women were not conscripted to work or serve in the armed forces; nevertheless, by the end of the war 1/3 of the industrial workforce was women. This gave women the opportunity to get better pay than they would have in their typical jobs such as domestic service.

The rationing from 1915 of bread soon saw other items soon follow; Germans consequently looked for alternatives. *Ersatz* coffee was made from tree bark, and *Ersatz* sausages contained no meat. For urban dwellers, the black market provided some relief; foraging visits (Hamsterfahrt) to 'relatives' in the country equally allowed greater access to food.

- The Hindenburg Programme

This marked the beginning of total war; the aim of the programme was to compensate for Germany's lack of raw materials through greater efficiency and drive. All Germany's resources would be mobilised for the war effort and non-essential industries shut down. The Supreme War Office was established to oversee the process of economic mobilisation, and the central pillar of the programme was the December 1916 Auxiliary Labour Law to mobilise all available labour for the war effort.

This made it compulsory for all German males between 17 and 60 to work for the war effort if required; a gesture to the trade unions was made in allowing unions to sit on boards that designated workers to various factories and mediate disputes in companies. Nevertheless, it was in all but name forced labour. It did have a significant impact on more munition production; from 6,100 machine guns in 1915 to 115,200 in 1917.

- 1916-8: problems on the Home Front

The shortages of fuel and raw materials were made worse by the desperately cold winter of 1916-7; coal production in 1917 was 90% of the production of 1913 and the freezing of railways and rivers made transportation of goods increasingly difficult. Local authorities, to cut down on fuel, dimmed street lights and cut back on trams. The potato harvest was destroyed – from 46m in 1914 to 30m in 1918. Livestock were destroyed, and in combination with the grain harvest poverty ensued with no food. Dairy production and animal fats fell by a third in 1917.

There was also a significant psychological impact; unlike any previous conflict, 16% of those conscripted had died (1.8m) – the families of those and millions more suffered physical and psychological disabilities.

These social problems affected social groups in different ways:

- Urban working classes

Had no access to cheap food; forced to turn to the turnip as an *Ersatz* potato – the 'Turnip Winter' of 1916-7 most affected the working classes. Local authorities set up soup kitchens to provide meals; 6,000,000 meals handed out in Hamburg in April alone. This was only temporary measure; since the bureaucracy failed to control the food supply, they could not effectively help the urban working classes. During the Turnip Winter, the average daily calories of food rations were 1,010 and only 13% of required fat intake. Thousands of deaths occurred from flu and hypothermia – 121,000 in 1916 and 293,000 in 1918.

The urban working classes resented the Polonaise (a slow dance, but nickname associated with queuing as a defining experience of the war), state controls, the black market where around a quarter of food was sold. They blamed the middle classes and in some cases the Jews.

- o The peasantry and rural producers

This group were alienated by government regulations; after having been hampered with a lack of labour in their work, they could either sell their grain for a fixed price or horde it. State prices were low and did not account production costs; they particularly resented the Junkers, who maintained their tax privileges until 1916 and the city war profiteers who seemed to make fortune out of the war.

- o The middle classes

Entered into insecurity without servants and savings worth less and less; the lower middle classes (the *Mittelstand*) such as teachers and officials experienced greater insecurity as the war closed the gap between those who were salaries and those who were not – the scarcity of food furthermore lessened their quality of life and perceived status in German society.

- o Impact of social discontent

This ultimately led to the political polarisation described above, as opposition to the war increased in combination with the perceived failure of the military conflict – especially after the American entry to the war and the failure of the final Ludendorff Offensive on the Western Front. Real earnings decreased by 25%, as £8394m was spent on a pointless conflict – the doctrines of nationalism and autocracy became less believable as the psychological trauma of the war became realised. A joke circulated, "Which family with six sons will survive the war?"

The political polarisation ultimately led to political change in 1918, with two revolutions, the abdication of the Kaiser and by 1919 the establishment of a new Weimar regime.

Change over time – the initial support of WWI

The anticipation of war had filled many Germans with dread; huge demonstrations were held from 28-9 July in Berlin, where crowds were 100,000 strong and across Germany. However, once the war had broken out there was a consensus considering national duty and patriotism.

Indeed, the war was presented by the government as a defensive campaign against Slav aggression. It was to be an easy and glorious victory as evidenced through expensive Naval laws, and in August military successes suggested German victory. On 4 August the Kaiser addressed the nation, telling the country "I know no parties any more, only Germans". Indeed, even the socialists in the Reichstag voted in favour of war credits – the political divisions of the pre-war era eased, and the Reichstag passed an Enabling Act on the same day known as Burgfrieden that re-enforced pre-war institutional challenges, rather than challenging them.

- The Reichstag delegated all its legislative powers to the Bundesrat, which would rule the Home Front through emergency legislation. The Reichstag could review such legislation, but not one of the 800 laws passed through the law were.

- The War Ministry took over the bureaucratic function of running the war; corporations were set up under its control to supply some raw materials for the war effort

Nevertheless it could not be argued everyone had supported the war in the beginning.

- 14 of 110 socialists in the Reichstag argued against the war before accepting party discipline in August 1914; at the end of 1914, one SPD deputy Karl Liebknecht voted against war credits, and at the end of 1915 20 deputies did.
- Small numbers of pacifists organised in groups such as the German Peace League, but these were marginal and had no real impact
- Radicals such as Liebknecht and Rosa Luxemburg spent most of the war in prison

d) Germany in 1918: revolutions

The 1917-8 failures saw discontent through the rise of the USPD, the July Crisis and the Peace Resolution of the Reichstag; in January 1918, a series of huge strikes gripped Berlin and other industrial centres saw over 1m workers take part; the leadership of the SPD and the trade unions aimed to seize the opportunity for an end to the war, more food and democratic rights. However, the Ludendorff Offensive saw Germany hold its breath and pause workers' discontent as they hoped victory might be sought.

However, the Ludendorff Offensive ultimately failed and Ludendorff sought armistice with the Allies and United States.

Revolution from above and return to parliamentary monarchy	
29 Sept	Ludendorff and Hindenburg recommend a new civilian government and an armistice
3 Oct	A new civilian government led by Prince Max of Baden, based on Reichstag support and coalition between liberals and socialists is formed
Revolution from below and the creation of a parliamentary republic	
2 Nov	Kiel sailors mutiny precipitates unrest
9 Nov	Prince Max hands over chancellorship to socialist leader Ebert; a republic is declared the Kaiser abdicates, fleeing to Holland.
10 Nov	The new socialist government makes an agreement with General Groener to gain the support of the army in protecting the government
Armistice	
11 Nov	The new government signs the armistice

The new government under Prince Max of Baden passed some reforms, but these were not sufficient to ease tensions and Germany erupted into a wave of unrest; it was at this point only that the Kaiser conceded to constitutional change:

- Reichstag could consider foreign and military affairs
- Democratic overhaul of the Prussian electoral system
- Cabinet government to be recognised by the constitution.

The prospect of defeat and peace sparked off mutiny in the naval ports of Wilhelmshaven on 29 Oct and Kiel on 2 Nov. The mutiny spread to other ports as sailors refused to fight the Royal Navy only as a suicide mission; councils of workers and soldiers called soviets were set up in towns and ports.

This sparked further unrest, with a Munich revolt on 8th November headed by socialist Kurt Eisner leading to the proclamation of a socialist democratic republic in Bavaria.

The Allies, as a condition of armistice, demanded that the Kaiser abdicate; this call was taken up by Prince Max's government, and the Kaiser fled to Holland. Nevertheless, the SPD withdrew support for Prince Max's government and Friedrich Ebert of the SPD became Chancellor of a new government consisting only of members of the USPD and SPD.

Before the Treaty of Versailles had been agreed, the armistice had other major conditions:

- The German army was to withdraw east of the Rhine.
- The Treaty of Brest-Litovsk (Russia, March 1918) and Treaty of Bucharest (Romania, May 1918) were to be renounced with German troops withdrawn from Russia, Romania, Austria-Hungary and Turkey.
- Germany was to surrender 150 submarines and several large naval vessels.

3. Weimar Republic 1919-23: formation and problems

a) Formation of the new Republic
b) The Treaty of Versailles
c) The Weimar Constitution
d) The Spartacist Revolt and Red Bavaria
e) The Kapp Putsch and paramilitary Freikorps
f) The threat of left versus right
g) Financial crisis: reparations and hyperinflation

a) Formation of the new Republic

A new state was born against background of national humiliation, forced to accept responsibility for the war and faced with a spectrum of domestic opposition and economic crises; together with the judiciary questioning the very legitimacy of the democratic Republic and paramilitary groups actively undermining it.

Ebert and forming Weimar

With peace declared the Kaiser abdicated, President Ebert's primary task was to ensure political stability. On 25 November 1918, a conference of representatives of the new state governments across Germany agreed to elections for a National Constituent Assembly. The USPD challenged the prospect of democratic elections, and hoped for workers to seize power; the more moderate 'majority SPD' favoured democracy.

The Ebert-Groener agreement was made in November 1918; the support of the army was by no means guaranteed given its traditionalist stances. Ebert made an agreement with General Groener as the threat of revolution from communist Spartacists was clear. Ebert promise the army supplies and protection of status against militias of workers' councils, and in return the army promised to put down revolutionary activity with force.

Elections to the new National Assembly were held on the 19th of January 1919. Participation in the election was high, with 85% of those eligible voting. The election was a triumph for the moderate parties – the SPD, Centre Party and DDP with three parties together gaining 77% of the vote, and the SPD with 38% alone. The USPD, by contrast, won just 8%.

b) The Treaty of Versailles

The abdication of the Kaiser and democratic elections in January 1919 led to the hope among Germans that the country would be treated leniently and that the final peace settlement would be based on President Woodrow Wilson's Fourteen Points.

The Peace Conference at Versailles opened on 18 January 1919; the victorious Allies and the US, without the Central Powers or Germany, debated the future of Germany and Europe. France, the UK, the US and Italy were the most influential as the so-called Council of Four. They together agreed:

- The League of Nations to be established for a peaceful European future (US)
- A Carthaginian peace – particularly harsh to stop Germany trying again (France)
- Accept responsibility for outbreak of war and pay reparations (France, UK)

The treaty was presented to a horrified German delegation in May 1919. Rather than accept the treaty, Chancellor Scheidemann of the SPD (who took the Chancellorship from February 1919, leaving Ebert President) resigned. The replaced government, with no military or economic means to resist an Allied invasion, was forced to accept the treaty on the 28th of June.

The conditions of the Treaty of Versailles included:

- Provisions of lost territory
- Military reductions
- War guilt and reparations

Provisions of lost territory

- Lost territory of economic importance (20% of coal production; 15% of agricultural resources)
- Lost territory of symbolic importance (West Prussia, Posen given to Poland where the majority population were German speakers)
- Created a feeling that the West was hypocritical in upholding self-determination of the peoples of Europe but not the Germans

- The Rhineland was to become a demilitarised zone as a buffer between France and Germany (15 years)
- Anschluss (union with Austria) forbidden by Article 80
- All Germany's colonies to be handed over to Allies, and whoever governs would be decided through the League of Nations.

Military terms

- Germany's military capacity was destroyed – the army limited to 100,000 men and the Navy to six battleships, six cruisers and twelve destroyers with no submarines
- No military aircraft

War guilt and reparations

- The Allies demanded, given the huge cost of war for them, that the Germans ought to pay some of the cost – given it had been decided they were responsible for the outbreak (Article 231)
- All countries had borrowed heavily from the USA; in 1923, the French were calculated to owe the Americans $4bn.
- While Wilson believed reparations should only be paid in compensation for breaking international law, such as the invasion of Belgium, the British and French were in favour of heavy reparations - in April 1919, Wilson conceded to these arguments.
- Reparations were not set until 1921; however, in the meantime Germany was to hand over many ships and build 200,000 tons of shipping a year for the Allies over five years.
- In April 1921, 132,000m gold marks were set for the next 30 years.

Was the treaty a Carthaginian peace?

While the treaty left Germany humiliated and scarred, it still left the country potentially strong with no limits on industrialisation and still a large, central European power. While not part of the League of Nations, it allowed for the potential to regain status as an important diplomatic power even in the short term – especially after the collapse of Imperial Russia power. This was shown by the Treaty of Rapallo in 1922 where both Germany and Russia rejecting reparations.

Versailles did not, indeed, limit Germany as much as enemies – especially the French – had wished. Far harsher was both the Brest-Litovsk Treaty with Russia in 1918 and the 1945 settlement with Germany.

The reaction within Germany: undermining the Republic

Virtually the whole German nation rejected the Treaty of Versailles; the nationalist newspaper *Deutsche Zeitung* proclaimed "death rather than slavery". Germans had expected victory, and even then the Fourteen Points posed by the USA that every nation has a right to govern itself were far more palatable. Germany was excluded from negotiations about the Treaty. The democratic Republic was seen as weak in accepting the conditions, and this led to a rise of the "stab in the back" myth.

The "stab in the back" myth purported by Hindenburg rejected that German military failures led to defeat in WWI, and instead blamed it on enemies at home who had undermined the military effort. In being unpatriotic, the post-revolution government, which was largely Jewish, had given into an unnecessary armistice and the humiliating Diktat (dictated to Germany without negotiation) Treaty of Versailles. This view was quickly used to criticise the Weimar Republic and the 'November criminals', including President Ebert.

Such accusations provided a psychological framework in which millions of German people could accept defeat, hence became widespread. Moreover, it gave the anti-Republican right-wing of Germany a moral justification for illegal and violent actions.

c) The Weimar Constitution

In the midst of the failure in World War One and the collapse of autocracy, together with the 1918 revolutions, a new constitution was to be created. In January 1919 a cross-party group from the new National Assembly was created to consider the possibilities. Many questions were to be posed.

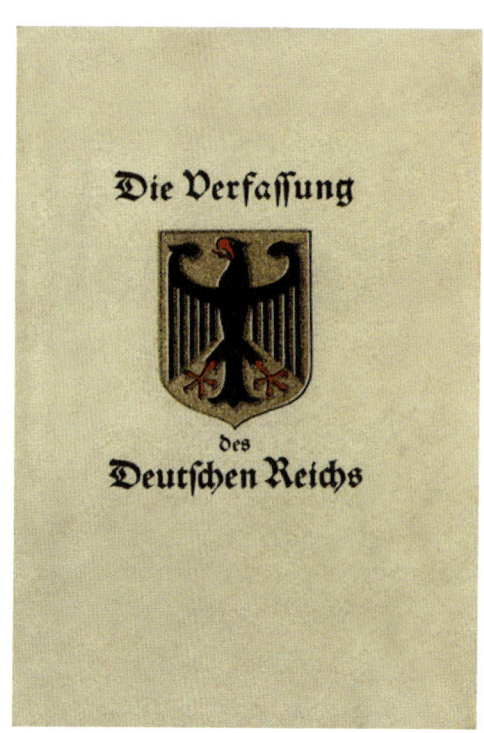

Hugo Preuss, a liberal lawyer and democrat given responsibility for writing the constitution itself, aimed to build on the traditions of German politics while balancing the power between different institutions of the state. After much discussion, the Weimar Constitution was adopted on 31 July 1919. It can be seen as one of the most significant factors for Weimar being doomed from the beginning.

The most significant aspects of the new Constitution were:

- Reichstag proportional representation and universal adult suffrage
- The retaining of autocratic elements, e.g. President and Article 48
- The federal nature of the Constitution.

Weaken the Republic	Did not weaken the Republic
Proportional Representation	
Every party receives one seat for every 60,000 cast for that party through lists rather than specific candidates. All men and women over 20 could vote.	
<ul><li>Created unstable and weak coalitions – 21 governments, 13 Chancellors. There were 7 Chancellors between 1919-23 alone.</li><li>Some coalitions were fundamentally unworkable in the long term, e.g. SPD + Zentrum</li><li>Proportional Representation partly responsible for rise of Hitler; NSDAP could gain more and more seats, catalysing its influence and keep walking out the Reichstag to cause re-elections</li><li>Exacerbated political polarisation; no clear party in power for example in 1919; SPD 38%, Centre 20%, DDP 19%, DNVP 10% - SPD had the largest portion with 165/423 seats but still easily defeated.</li></ul>	<ul><li>Allowed for a wider representation of interests in the context of a socially divided Germany. Since the Chancellor had to listen to the Reichstag, this allowed for effective coalitions. (but... autocracy and Bruning?)</li><li>No more Putschs / coups – less violence directed against the state, and legalism used by extreme parties which might have made them more docile in general, lessening their influence; Hitler's rise was not inevitable.</li><li>While coalitions may have changed, many government minsters remained constant. For example Strassman was foreign minister 1923-9, and fairly moderate with achievements from Rapallo, League of Nations Entry, the Locarno Pact etc.)</li></ul>

Retaining of Autocracy	
- A strong executive, with a tenure of 7 years, was given significant powers – including that of appointing and dismissing the Chancellor, which ultimately led to the appointment of Hitler as Chancellor in January 1933 by President Hindenburg. - Article 48 gave the Chancellor the power to rule by decree during "emergencies", without defining what one was. With no clear parliamentary majority evident often due to PR, this led to autocratic use of the clause. Under Bruning's government from March 1930, Hindenburg had made it clear that if the minority government was defeated or lost a vote of no confidence, then the Reichstag would be dissolved and Article 48 would be used. After being defeated comprehensively in July 1930 over its Finance Bill, the government despite the Reichstag condemning it passed it by decree. By 1932, 115 emergency decrees had been issued by Bruning, and in 1932 only 5 laws were passed by the Reichstag compared with 66 by decree.	- Bruning's ability to take hold of the situation and handle the finances through austerity, arguably, led to the economic recovery at the beginning of 1933 – nevertheless, Weimar had already fallen by then and Hitler could take credit for the recovery. - Article 48 allowed the government the strength to put down major threats to the Weimar Republic – President Ebert used it during the Nov 1923 Munich Putsch to give power to the army to put it down; indeed, from the period 1919-23 it gave sufficient power to the government to defend the Republic. - Germany, in its desire for a "strong man" leader, was not ready for democracy and perhaps better suited to the retaining of more autocratic elements in the constitution to help lead the country in a tangible direction.
Federal nature of Constitution	
- Allowed regions (the Länder) to deal with much of their own affairs including police, allowing for a localised control; checks and balances ensured that no one group within any part of the government dominated the system. There was also regional influence in the Parliament, with representation of Länder nominees in the national second chamber, the Reichsrat.	- The federal government could still fundamentally exert control over the Länder, rendering this aspect of the constitution superfluous. In July 1932, the Prussian coup saw Hindenburg issue an emergency decree under Article 48 of the Weimar Constitution which dismissed the cabinet of the Free State of Prussia, the largest German state ostentatiously over Prussia's inability to handle internal violence, but in actuality because Prussia's police force was one of the last major forces against von Papen's intended nationalist and centrist government. This further helped Hitler's advance to power, facilitating the NSDAP's "Gleichschaltung" (Evans: forcible coordination).

d) The Spartacist Revolt and Red Bavaria

In the midst of a new government, in December 1918 a group of revolutionaries led by Karl Liebknecht and Rosa Luxemburg broke away from the USPD; their aspirations were revolutionary and inspired by the Russian Bolshevism of 1917, with all power transferred from the new National Assembly to workers' and soldiers' councils, and the nationalisation of all industries.

On 1 January 1919, members of the Spartacist Union held their first Congress in Berlin and with the support of other left wing groups formed the German Communist Party, the KPD. This was followed by a revolutionary uprising beginning 5 January 1919, despite the Ebert-Groener agreement signed in November 1918.

- Newspaper offices were seized and revolutionary committees formed
- But the uprising was poorly planned and easily crushed by troops from both the regular army which supported the government and the Freikorps
- On 15 January, members of the House Guards Division of the army murdered Liebknecht and Luxemburg

While the actions of the army may have saved Germany from a communist uprising, the alliance came at a price to the new government; they were now tied to using anti-democratic forces such as the army and Freikorps. This is further evidenced through the situation in Bavaria during 1919.

Red Bavaria
In February 1919, Kurt Eisner – the USPD leader in Bavaria – was assassinated by a right-wing student. In conjunction with news from Hungary of Soviet revolution, communist revolution was triggered in Bavaria. On 6 April, the Bavarian Soviet Republic was declared – radical reforms such as seizing property from the wealthy were purported, with a Red Army of workers raised, rounding up well-known right-wingers and executing them. In early May 1919, the Army and Freikorps sent a force of 30,000 troops into Bavaria and crushed the movement – claiming 1,000 lives of the Red Army. When the fighting had ended, 800 known communists were rounded up and executed.

For many on the left, the SPD, Weimar and Ebert could no longer be trusted.

e) Kapp Putsch and paramilitary Freikorps

Kapp-Lüttwitz Putsch (1920)

The threats to the Republic were already evident in 1920; angered both by the socialist government, the democratic constitution and the humiliating Treaty of Versailles that not only made Germany accept responsibility but significantly reduce its military capacity, there was a movement to overthrow the Weimar state.

The figurehead of the movement was General Ludendorff, but other leaders were Wolfgang Kapp (from the right-wing Patriotic Party) and General von Lüttwitz of the Freikorps.

In March 1920, the government Defence Minister ordered that two brigades of the Freikorps disband to scale down the armed forces – a group of army officers refused and instead demanded the resignation of Ebert and dissolution of the Reichstag.

On the night of 12 March and morning of the 13th, Lüttwitz led his Freikorps brigade into Berlin where they seized the government district of the city; the Defence Minister Gustav Noske ordered the army to act. The Head of the General Staff, General von Seeckt, ordered his troops to stay in their barracks ordering that "Reichswehr does not fire on Reichswehr".

Consequently, Kapp was declared Chancellor by Lüttwitz; the government fled to Dresden but before it left it appealed to workers to defend the Republic. The response saw a large general strike that paralysed the capital and the rebels under Kapp failed to win support or recognition of the civil service or financial institutions including the Reichsbank. The Kapp regime collapsed after four days.

The Kapp Putsch posed a significant threat to the Republic, revealing the army's reluctance to support the Republic and the dubious loyalty of the Freikorps; indeed, only one army officer was imprisoned for his role in the plot. In Bavaria, army officer sympathetic to the Putsch forced the elected SPD state government to resign and replaced it with a government of the right. Clearly the event indicated the strength of the right and that the Republic relied nearly exclusively on unreliable forces to maintain any sense of order. Indeed, during the Ruhr Revolution of 1920, the government relied on the Freikorps and the Army to crush the attempt at a Soviet state.

f) The Threat of Left versus Right

The threat and balance between left and right ideology can be seen in the context of various axioms of political division:

- Parliamentary and governmental representation
- Governmental support: judiciary and the army
- Extra-constitutional movements

Parliamentary and governmental representation

Influence of the Left	Influence of the Right
- Consequent of the revolution from below. - SPD won 38% of vote in National Assembly elections in January 1919, and were involved in 6 of 8 coalitions from 1919 to 1923. - President Ebert was President from February 1919 to February 1925 - Much social welfare legislation passed: The Reich Insurance Code of May 1920 provided war-wounded persons with welfare and the Cripples' Welfare Act, passed that same month, made the public welfare system assist cripples under the age of 18 to earn income - Introduced unemployment insurance for all workers, trade union recognition and an eight-hour work day in 1918.	- SPD had major losses by 1920 after the Treaty of Versailles and the propagation of the 'stab in the back' myth, leading to a sense of anti-Republicanism and anti-democracy; hence in elections June 1920 – the USPD gained only 22% of the vote, and the USPD 18%. - The DVP was in 11 of 13 coalitions from 1920 to 1930. - Stresemann, foreign minister from 1923 to 1929, was part of the centre-right liberal DVP and fundamentally determined Germany's course of foreign policy through several coalitions. - Hindenburg became President from 1925 until 1934, allowing many on the Right to take office such as von Papen, who would later allow the rise of Hitler.

Governmental support: judiciary and army

Influence of the Left	Influence of the Right
- The Ebert-Groener agreement was made in November 1918; the support of the army was by no means guaranteed given its traditionalist stances. Ebert made an agreement with General Groener as the threat of revolution from communist Spartacists was	- The judiciary were born from a pre-war caste and their interpretations of law reveal their sympathies – by Article 54 of the Constitution, they maintained their independence, which was used to undermine the spirit of the constitution. - Plenty examples of judicial

clear. Ebert promise the army supplies and protection of status against militias of workers' councils, and in return the army promised to put down revolutionary activity with force • This fundamentally saw the army protect the SPD and the Weimar Republic from any threats. • Indeed, the army did step in during the Munich Putsch of 1923 eventually; Seeckt attempted to prevent a split in the army by acting in the interests of the Republic and in stopping the NSDAP. The Bavarian police equally saved the situation from the army having to fire against its own comrades and nationalists. • `The judiciary still did punish Hitler and criminals, if with lenient sentences. For example, Hitler was banned from speaking across most of Germany after his release.	neutrality being undermined. The role played by the judiciary in the case of Matthias Erzberger in early 1920 – accused by the leader of the DNVP of corruption and fraud, the court found against Erzberger in a decision that was dubious at best. In 1924, after the Munich Putsch, Adolf Hitler was given only five years for high treason during the trial – and was allowed to make dramatic speeches during the case against the Republic. • The army was also heavily right-wing. The attempts of the KPD for a German 'October Revolution' in 1923 failed because of a prompt deployment of Reichswehr units. • By contrast, the army's failure to stop the right-wing Kapp Putsch in 1920 and General von Seeckt's initial refusal to sent troops to the Munich coup in 1923 highlighted their sympathies for the Right.

Extra-constitutional movements / German society

Influence of the Left	Influence of the Right
• There was a significant fear of communist revolution, from the events of Kiel in November 1918 and in Bavaria April 1919. Indeed, revolution in Germany was a central element of Lenin's foreign policy • Red Bavaria • Spartacist Revolt • Stinnes-Legien Agreement (15 Nov 1918) – a compromise between workers and employers to protect workers' rights, with strong concessions from employees. Industrialists recognised the role of trade unions to undermine the prospect of socialisation of industry	• The Left was extremely divided: between the SPD (whom the Communists did not trust after the bourgeois events of 1919), the KPD and the USPD (which split in October 1920 to the other two); and moreover, it was unorganised. • Detail found elsewhere on: • Kapp Putsch • Munich Putsch • More organised and likely to become successful than those on the left given the army and courts' leniency. • Indeed, of the 376 political murders that took place between 1920-22, 354 were by the Right.

g) Financial crisis

Reparations 1919-23

Through the war guilt clause of the Treaty of Versailles, Germany had an obligation to pay for war damage. Between 1919 and 1921, 23 conferences were held to discuss the levels of reparations to be paid.

- The Spa Conference in July 1920 agreed on proportions of France (52%), Britain (22%), Italy (10%) and Belgium (8%)

- The Paris Conference in Jan 1921 decided on a figure of 226,000m gold marks; the German government rejected this as excessive and French troops occupied three major German cities.

- The London Conference in April 1921 saw the Reparations Committee set a new figure for 132,000m gold marks and 26% of exports value. Failure to agree or pay the first instalment would see the French invasion of the Ruhr.

- The German government resigned in protest and a new one under the leadership of Julian Wirth accepted the reparation terms on 11 May 1921 and raised a loan in London to pay the first instalment. The policy embarked on called fulfilment involved fulfilling the terms of the treaty so its terms could be seen as unjust and unworkable.

Hyperinflation

All nations involved in the war had struggled with coming to grips with economic readjustment and debt; Germany was no different, seeing its currency collapse in 1923. Reparations made matters worse; in 1919 the national debt stood at 144m marks, yet by late 1922 it had increased to 469m marks. The Republic was set on a course for hyperinflation.

In June 1922, the government asked permission to suspend further reparation payments. This was refused by the French Prime Minister who demanded many conditions of 'productive guarantees', including the state mines of the Ruhr. The German government chose simply to print more money to cover its debts; this was seen by the Allies as a deliberate sabotage of reparations. In late 1922, the Reparations Commission – amidst German financial disaster – declared that Germany failed to deliver the promised coal and timber to the Allies.

Bread prices in marks indicated the trend of hyperinflation:

1918	Jan 1923	Sep 1923	Nov 1923
0.63	250	1,500m	201,000m

Ruhr Crisis, 1923

The Germans defaulting on their reparations led to the French/Belgian occupation of the Ruhr in January 1923 with 60,000 troops. The German government encouraged the workers to offer passive resistance, a refusal to work or cooperate with the occupiers, in outrage. France and Belgium responded by arresting mine owners and taking over the mines and railways

While passive resistant reduced the amount of coal delivered to France and Belgium, the government nevertheless had to pay millions of marks to those who lost revenue as a result. The lack of income meant the government simply printed even more money – by August 1923 there were 663bn (,000,000,000,000) marks in circulation.

Consequently, the currency and the policy of passive resistance collapsed. The economy also collapsed; by the end of 1923, only 29% of trade union members worked full time. This shook the faith of many Germans in the Republic: the middle classes saw their savings destroyed, and the working class were either out of work or saw their wages fall in real terms.

Stabilisation of currency

In August 1923, a new government led by Stresemann was formed and took measures to stabilise the situation. In September, payments of reparations were resumed and the French agreed to establish a commission to study the problem of the German economy. In November, the Rentenmark was established by the Finance Minister to replace the old mark with printing strictly limited. The Minister also sacked 700,000 state employees to attempt to balance the budget.

Conclusions

Early threats to the Republic:
Was the Weimar Republic doomed to fail?

- The Weimar Constitution – instability and autocracy
- The Treaty of Versailles humiliation and Reparations; Ruhr crisis
- The political polarisation between Left and Right; both opposed to Weimar – the isolation and weakness of governments
    - The Right, and the "stab in the back" myth
        - Extra-constitutional movements: Kapp/Munich Putsch; Freikorps
        - The army and the Ebert-Groener Pact
        - The judiciary
        - The government 1923/5-
    - The Left, and disunity within
        - The oft-governing SPD resentment: bourgeois-democratic Ebert
        - The USPD and KPD disunity amidst the 1917 October Revolution
        - The Spartacist Revolt and Red Bavaria
        - A serious threat?
            - Little support, especially in rural areas; disunity within the movement; a lack of paramilitary power; fear from the middle classes precipitated anti-communist action
- Poor economic management – hyperinflation

Example exam questions

1. 'The main threat to the stability of the Weimar Republic in the period 1919 to 1923 came from the political violence of the extreme right.' How far do you agree with this judgment?
2. 'The main threat to the existence of the Weimar Republic in the years 1919-1923 was its fated constitution' How far do you agree with this judgement?
3. Why did the Weimar Republic survive despite significant threats to its existence during the years 1919-23?

4. Weimar 1924-29: Stresemann Years and stability

a) Political Stalemate 1924-5
b) Reparations: The Dawes and Young Plans
c) Political Polarisation and Instability 1926-30

The Golden Years?
d) German Economy 1924-9
e) German Society 1924-9
f) German Culture 1924-9
g) German Politics summary 1924-9
h) Foreign policy and Stresemann

Bundesarchiv, Bild 102-08490
Foto: o.Ang. | 10. September 1926

a) The Political Stalemate of 1924-5

The mid-years of the Weimar Republic did not see extra-parliamentary action typified between 1918-23. Nevertheless, the period can hardly be seen as fundamentally stable – parliamentary democracy was still widely resented and failed to develop. A primary reason for this was the failure of proportional representation to produce governments with sufficient support to tackle the problems that faced the new democracy. While the currency had been stabilised by 1924, the financial crisis remained – while some had massively lost on savings and wages, industrialists gained by paying workers less.

Frequent political paralysis transcended from the partisan environment of proportional representation; the DVP's increasingly strong association with industrial and business interest saw refusal to enter coalition with the SPD in 1926. The inability of successive coalitions to act or legislate meant that the structural shortfalls of cultural, political and economic Weimar were not addressed cohesively.

Post-hyperinflation: Election May 1924

Stresemann's government lacked the support of a Reichstag majority and consequently collapsed in late November 1923; nevertheless, Stresemann continued as Foreign Minister. The effect of hyperinflation and economic uncertainty saw extreme parties gain at the expense of the moderate parties of the centre:

Party	% of votes	Seats
Zentrum	13%	210
SPD	21%	
DVP	9%	
NSDAP	6.5%	189
KPD	13%	
DNVP	20%	

Election December 1924

The SPD saw a change in fortunes, gaining 31 seats to have a total of 131 with 26% of the vote. There was a dip in extremist groups - the NSDAP's vote dropped to 3%, and the KPD's to 9%, while the DNVP's remained constant.

1924-8: Coalition Obstruction by the SPD

A new coalition in 1925 was led by Hans Luther; the coalition excluded socialists but included the nationalist DNVP; the DNVP objected to the terms of the Locarno treaties negotiated by Stresemann, passed in November 1925 only because of the support from the SPD. The SPD refused to enter into coalitions with bourgeois parties (DDP, Centre or DVP) – this exacerbated the problems of proportional representation causing coalitions.

Indeed, despite being the largest party in the Reichstag, between early 1924 and June 1928 the SPD resisted becoming involved in forming viable coalition governments. It argued it did not want to compromise its ideals with bourgeois parties. This was strengthened through the consolidation of Marxist ideals at the 1925 party conference of the Heidelberg Programme that would transfer means of production to social owners. As the major party only gave tacit support to governments such as that of Wilhelm Marx (of the Centre Party) in 1926, they failed to past long and the SPD obstructed its own influence. Constructive political census was thereafter unlikely.

1925: Election of Hindenburg

The stalemate of 1924-5 was reinforced by the election of President Hindenburg to office on 26 April 1925. He won the election due a split in the left vote between the Centre Party and the KPD, nevertheless obtaining 14.6m votes. He made it clear he would not accept SPD participation in a coalition government. While he was tied by his oath as President to protect the Constitution, his election had a huge impact on how the constitution and democracy operated.

From the moment of his election, he worked tirelessly not only to create coalitions that would exclude the SPD – this made it difficult for parties to find coalition partners; nevertheless, when the SPD did enter coalition – such as the Müller government that was formed in June 1928 – it was beset with problems. Hindenburg was sure to avoid limitations to his power. In 1926 the Ministry of the Interior produced a draft law defining the use of Article 48, but Hindenburg blocked the draft law from proceeding.

b) Reparations: the Dawes and Young Plans

The Dawes Plan (1924)

Stresemann believed that a policy of fulfilment was the best course of action in dealing with the Allies; Germany's need for raw materials and restoration of confidence in the economy were factors in this. He therefore willingly collaborated with the Americans in considering the issue of reparations – the Dawes Plan was put together by a committee of economists and in April 1924 produced proposals:

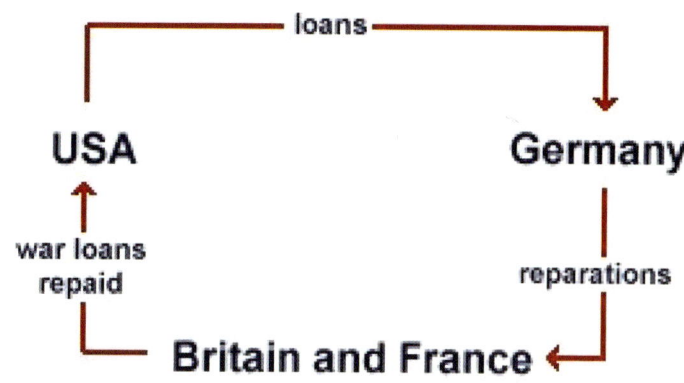

- The French would leave the Ruhr

- Reparations would be paid over a longer period of time, and credit advanced to help rebuild the German economy. An international loan of 800m Reichsmarks would be covered to grant 4/5 of reparation payments of 1,000m Reichmarks a year. The higher level of 2,500 would be paid after 1929.

- The reparations would be paid in such a way as not to threaten the stability of the German currency, with the Reichsbank to be reorganised under Allied supervision.

The US fundamentally bailed out Germany. However, Chancellor Wilhelm Marx had to pass the Dawes Plan through the Reichstag; the main problem involved was getting MPs to accept they had to continue to pay reparations. The collapse of the SPD vote in May 1924 (from 171 to 100 seats) made the task of finding a two-third majority even harder. Nevertheless, the Plan was approved in August 1924 with the support of the DNVP – while often opposing Versailles and democracy, needed to appease constituents.

The Young Plan (1929)

In June 1928, a ministry dominated by socialists was formed, led by Hermann Müller and including members of the DDP, DVP, Centre Party and BVP; the main task of this 'grand coalition' was to steer through the Reichstag the Young Plan of 1929. Under the terms of the Dawes Plan, Germany was due to pay reparations at a higher rate from 1929.

In September 1928, the Müller government requested that France evacuate the Rhineland; the French were only prepared to consider this alongside plans for future payments of reparations. The Young Plan included the following proposals:

- The timescale for the repayment of reparations was set – Germany was to make payments for the next 59 years until 1988 – it was to pay 2,000m marks a year, rather than the 2,500m laid out under the Dawes Plan.

- Responsibility for paying reparations was passed to Germany; exchange of payments into other currencies was to be handled by a new institution in Switzerland.

- Payments were to increase gradually and, from 1929 to 1932, Germany would pay 1,700m marks less than it would have paid under Dawes

Consequently, the French promised to evacuate the Rhineland by June 1930, five years ahead of schedule – an important diplomatic victory for Stresemann.

The Freedom Law: 1929 attempt to end reparations

Despite concessions won by Stresemann in negotiation of the Young Plan, German politicians were not impressed – particularly incensed by the fact Germany still had to pay reparations. Under Article 73 of the Constitution, it was possible to petition for a referendum. The leader of the DNVP Hugenberg organised a petition that raised some four million signatures; the campaign included Adolf Hitler. It was enough fro a referendum that demanded the repudiation of Article 231 of Versailles; held on the 22nd December 1929; only 14% of those who voted, however, voted to support the Freedom Law despite the campaign. The Young Plan was, hence, passed in March 1930 with the overshadowing of the Wall St Crash in October 1929.

c) The Political Polarisation and Instability of 1926-30

Several governments between 1926-7 were formed and fell:

Jan 1926 Hans Luther (Z, DVP, DNVP)	Instruction to the country's diplomatic corps to use the old imperial flag	Reichstag vote of no confidence in May 1926
June 1926 Wilhelm Marx (Z, DVP, DNVP, tacit support of SPD)	Referendum on the confiscation of royal property, failing to reach required majority	SPD removed support in late 1926
Jan 1927 Wilhelm Marx + DNVP (Z, DNVP, BVP, DVP)	Social legislation passed – including comprehensive form of unemployment insurance (July 1927)	The coalition collapsed February 1928 over the issue of religion in education.

May 1928 election

The left made significant gains in this election: the SPD increased its share of seats by 22 to 153 and the KPD showed a rise of 9 seats to 54. The parties of the centre and right saw their vote decline; by the time the SPD was prepared to form a coalition after their election victory, the political polarisation meant forming a stable majority government had become virtually impossible. The SPD and the KPD together gained 40% of the vote.

DNVP moves right

Extremes in German politics predated the Wall Street Crash; a very good example of drift to extremes was the changing nature of the DNVP from a party covering a broad coalition of groups to one with a narrow anti-Republican and anti-democratic outlook. The publication of the Lambach Article in 1928 was the trigger for a shift in policy – the piece urged DNVP members to reconcile nostalgic monarchism and consider the permanence of the Republic; there was such a backlash that Alfred Hugenberg was elected leader in October 1928 on a strongly anti-democratic platform.

Collapse of the grand coalition

Much of the economic recovery of the mid 1920s and relied on short-term loans form abroad, especially the United States. As the Depression deepened, those who lent money demanded repayment the unemployment system saw increasing strain with unemployment rising in the late 1920s – employers increasingly protested the increasing cost of social security payments. By 1929 the Reich Institution was forced to borrow money from the government to pay for the benefits for the 3.6m unemployed people (having had 1.3m unemployed two years before. This split the parties, with the SPD arguing the employers should increase their contribution to the fund by 4%, while the DVP said contributions should not be increased but rather benefits cut. The mediating Centre Party negotiated a deal where the decision would be put of until autumn 1930.

In March 1930 the SPD rejected the Centre Party's compromise and brought down Müller's government – this was indicative of the narrowing interests of the mainstream parties that would be a cause of their decline, with voters looking to parties of the extreme.

Weimar 1924-9: the "Golden Years"?

d) German Economy 1924-9: did it improve?

- ✓ <u>Significant monetary stability</u> – which was particularly important in the aftermath of the hyperinflation crisis. Due to the establishment of the Rentenmark by Stresemann in 1924 and Dawes Plan; a significant influx of foreign capital, 26bn marks, between 1924 and 1930 enabling the reconstruction of German industry but making Germany reliant on the economic stability of other countries

- ✓ <u>Delay of reparation payments</u> – the growth in available capital due to the delaying of payments thereby stimulating some inward capital investment (paying only 1,000m marks per year until 1929). National income was 12% higher in 1928 than in 1913 and industry experienced significant growth.

- ✓ <u>Industrial growth</u> – production reached pre-war levels in 1927, and then surpassed this level by 26% in the following year. Equally, real wages increased for workers by approx. 30% from 1924-9

- ✗ <u>Agricultural problems</u> – agriculture was fairly backward, with a failure to modernise and widespread rural poverty due the global collapse in food prices from 1922. Indeed, in the mid 1920s, the agricultural output was only recorded to be 76% of that of pre-war levels in 1913. This was significantly damaging to the German farmers and the lower middle class (Mittelstand), who would be the first to turn to extremist parties such as the NSDAP

- ✗ <u>Unemployment</u> – 6% in 1924, peak 11% 1926 and then 8% in 1929 – peaked during these years, however paled in comparison to the massive unemployment of the era afterwards

- ✗ <u>Industrial unrest</u> – while the period was one of economic growth, it was not one of stability – especially in terms of industrial relations.

    - The mid 1920s saw an increasingly concerted attack by employers on the rights of labour. In 1923, the legislation of 1918 that enforced an eight hour day was altered to allow a ten hour day in some circumstances.
    - Unions demanded for higher wages, with 76,000 cases between 1924 to 1932; employers resented such procedure, and in late 1928 in the Ruhr ironworks owners locked over 210,000 workers rather than accept the findings of arbitration.

e) German Society 1924-9: did it change?

- ✓ Welfare state – this was enshrined in the constitution: the family should lay at the centre of German life, it was the responsibility of adults to protect and nurture young people, religious freedom was guaranteed. Moreover, there was an inclusive welfare state that had been made ever greater by the impact of the war.

- ✓ The Reich Relief Law and the Serious Disability Laws, all passed in 1920 provided the framework for support. In 1924 the system for claiming relief and assessing the needs of the claimants was codified; 1927 the Labour Exchanges and Unemployment Insurance Law introduced unemployment insurance, which became an important political issue. From 15% of GNP in 1913, by the late 1920s, 26% went to social causes.

- ✓ Housing and public health – public spending on housing grew rapidly through the 1920s; by 1929 the state was spending 33 times more on housing than it had been in 1913. The effect was to provide better quality homes for many Germans, which in turn lowered the amount of death from diseases. Deaths from tuberculosis decreased from 143 in every 10,000 to 87 in every 10,000 from 1913 to 1928; in the same time period, 63 hospital beds per 10,000 Germans to 91.

- ✓ Women – There were growing numbers of women in areas of employment such as the civil service, teaching or social work. They were formally emancipated in a welfare state.

- ✓ Youth – The Weimar Stat intervened in an attempt to improve the upbringing of the nation's children; the Reich Youth Law of 1922 claimed the right of all children to a decent upbringing. But this was a difficult claim to fulfil in reality.

- ✗ Women – The proportion of women who worked outside the home during the Weimar period remained roughly the same as before 1914; the jobs they did were also fairly similar; there was little change in the numbers of domestic servants or farm workers. Indeed, attitudes towards women working remained generally conservative with 65% still unemployed – those in 'men's jobs' during the war gave up this work in 1918; from 1924, there was increasing condemnation of 'Doppelverdiener' (second earners) – married women – as businesses saw men laid off. This criticism became even sharper during the depression.

- ✗ Old institutions – Protestant and Catholic churches and schools propagated anti-democratic, conservative ideas – repugnance of moral decadence.

f) German Culture 1924-9: did it develop?

- ✓ <u>Liberation and modernity</u>

- ✓ New communications of film and radio – More entertainment allowed that broke class divisions, and eroded the hold of the SPD on organisations of the working class. Cinema and theatre dominated by plays that reflected social issues with seriousness; for example several works (typically nationalist) on the First World War, but some quite the opposite – for example the pacifist literature *All Quiet on the Western Front* published 1928. But also used against liberation – in 1932, von Papen asserted political control over the radio.

- ✓ Architecture and the Arts – Architecture became dominated by the Bauhaus movement; this stressed the relationship between art and technology, with functionality of design and freedom from the past. The architecture was very modern, and new house designs in towns and cities saw only small living spaces rather than those oriented to a family environment.

- ✓ Neue Sachlichkeit and Weimar disenchantment – a new matter of fact style to expose the weaknesses and injustices of Weimar society developed in the mid 1920s. It indicated a significant portion of society opposed and disenchanted with Weimar.

- ✓ Cultural expression – an explosion of culture; mainly in Berlin:

    a. Swing music and dance
    b. Acceptance of women smoking; gender equality
    c. Homosexuality more acceptable
    d. Transvestism and cross dressing
    e. Increased drug use

- ✗ <u>Conservative continuity</u>

- ✗ What can be popularly described, as 'Weimar culture' was only manifestation of cultural expression; in reality, the traditional taste of the majority population differed sharply from modernism and liberalism.

- ✗ Escapism – many writers on the political right contributed to an anti-democratic German literature glorifying the experiences of WWI. A culture that rejected the objectivity of *Neue Sachlichkeit* and found refuge in escapism; authors such as Hans Grimm saw increasing sales. In cinema escapism found expression in films such as that of Charlie Chaplin.

- Repugnance for moral decadence – Fritz Haarmaan, who killed and sodomised 27 young male prostitutes by biting their necks ("the vampire of Hannover") was an image of moral decadence in Berlin and Weimar for traditionalists – homosexuality, sodomy, homelessness, regression from family values; the same messages utilised by the NSDAP. This caused a moral friction between Germany and Berlin; Weimar was Berlin, Berlin Weimar – but where was the Reich?

g) German Politics 1924-9: summary

✓ <u>Policy successes</u>
- Social welfare legislation passed in the 1920s
- Reparations negotiation: Young and Dawes Plan
- Continuity of Stresemann as Foreign Minister 1923-9 and successes

✗ <u>Ineffectiveness of Weimar Constitution for effective government</u>
- Continuous coalition governments that came and fell, e.g. 1926
- Article 48 and the overly powerful President Hindenburg interference
- Federalism and the Prussian coup

✗ <u>Nazi Party developing underneath</u>
- Hitler writes "Mein Kampf" in prison while factional splits damage NSDAP
- Establishment of Fuhrer Party and reorganisation
- Popularity and successes in rural areas; electoral success increases

✗ <u>Polarisation</u>
- Extremist parties in election post-hyperinflation
- Election of Hindenburg to President, despite SPD largest party
- SPD obstruction of coalition government 1924-8
- May 1928 election and DNVP shift to the right
- Collapse of grand coalition

h) Foreign Policy and Stresemann: a success?

- ✓ **Better relations with the Allies** – From 1919 to 1924, relations were poor with Versailles, and Germany's Rapello agreement in 1922 with Russia together with the Ruhr crisis. There were several reasons for changes – the election of a Labour government in Britain in 1924 produced a friendly attitude towards Germany which was later maintained, equally the left's electoral victory in France saw a government far more open to constructive dialogue. Stresemann could hence negotiate more diplomacy. In 1926, the allied occupation forces were reduced by 60,000 – a relationship that gradually bettered through the period.

- ✓ **Locarno** – A diplomatic priority was the evacuation of French from the Rhineland; in October 1925, the treaty included mutual agreement of borders and the agreement not to use force to alter these. Stresemann was even able to negotiate from France a guarantee it would not attack Germany in a Polish-German war where Germany was not the aggressor. Nevertheless, France only withdrew some troops and it took the Young Plan just before Stresemann's death for the Allies to evacuate the Rhineland in 1930.

- ✓ **League of Nations** – Germany's exclusion from the LoN from 1919 at its creation had meant it could not revise Versailles from within its structures; the Locarno agreements allowed Germany's admission in 1926.

- ✓ **Relations with Soviet Union** – In April 1926, the Treaty of Berlin was signed between the USSR and Germany which reconfirmed the terms of the Treaty of Rapallo by stressing neutrality in a third power attack.

- ✓ **Fulfilment** – significant progress was made in the policy of 'fulfilment', i.e. fulfilling the terms of Versailles to show it as unworkable and unjust.

- ✓ **Reparations** – Dawes and Young Plan were successes for Germany – strengthened Germany's industrial bases and revised the reparations payments in the long term respectively.

- ✗ **Failure to result in domestic stability** – with no actual revision of the Versailles treaty, and a large section of German society still hostile to the Allies, Stresemann was not recognised universally as successful in the domestic sphere. The stab in the back myth and reparations continued to undermine Weimar, e.g. 1929 referendum on Freedom Law – 5.8m Germans rejected Stresemann's policy and labelled him a traitor

- ✗ **Lack of manoeuvre** – Versailles undermined Germany's military capacity, so Stresemann had little option but to follow the route of peaceful policy and diplomacy – indeed the gradual approach allowed for extremist opposition.

Summary Table: Weimar 1924-9, the "Golden Years"?

Yes: "Golden Years"

Society	Culture	Economics	Politics	Foreign
Welfare state	New communications of film and radio	Monetary stability	Policy successes	Better relations with Allies
Housing and public health	Architecture and the Arts	Delay in reparation repayments		Locarno and Allied evacuation
Women	Neue Sachlichkeit	Industrial growth		League of Nations
Youth	Cultural expression			USSR
				Fulfilment and reparations

No: not the "Golden Years"

Society	Culture	Economics	Politics	Foreign
Women	Escapism	Agricultural failures	Ineffectiveness of Weimar constitution	Failure of domestic support
Old institutions	Moral decadence	Unemployment	NSDAP blossoming	Lack of manoeuvre
		Industrial unrest	Polarisation	

Example exam questions

1. To what extent could the period 1924 to 1929 be described as one of economic, social and cultural stability?
2. "Germany experienced a period of political calm, economic development and social progress in the mid-1920s." How far do you agree with this judgement?

5. The Development of the Nazi Party 1920-9

a) Nazis' Foundations and the Munich Putsch
b) Reorganisation and development of NSDAP

a) Nazis' foundations and the Munich Putsch

- Anton Drexler founded the German Workers' Party in 1919 against a background of political turmoil in the new Weimar Republic; Hitler and Drexler together wrote the Twenty-Five Point programme in 1920 as the party assumed a new name, the National Socialist German Workers' Party.

- The themes of the document remained fairly constant: the revision of Versailles, the ending of reparations, the creation of a *Lebensraum* (living space) for the German people, a Volksgemeinschaft (national community) and anti-Semitism.

- The party became one of the more noticeable among the many splinter fringe groups on the right. In December 1920, the increase in membership meant it could run its own newspaper, the People's Observer. In the following three years, Hitler consolidated his leadership of and influence of the party becoming chairman of the party in July 1921.

- This was followed by the creation of the SA (storm troopers) that would become the paramilitary group in the party, primarily aimed at street violence with communist.

Munich Putsch 1923 (or Beer Hall Putsch)

- By mid-1923, the party had 55,000 members from just 3,300 in 1921. Many of whom attracted to the radical nationalism and "catch all" manifesto; the Ruhr Crisis of 1923 propagated the discontent of the Weimar Republic. A failed attempt of direct action in May saw tension between the Reich and the Bavaria government about the latter's failure to arrest nationalists together with the crisis of hyperinflation and discontent of the French Ruhr occupation saw the Nazis interpret this as the right time to seize power.

- The aim of the uprising was to place General Ludendorff as President; the attempted coup in November, however, saw 17 dead and the arrest of Hitler.

- Herman Göring, a well-known WWI fighter pilot hero, joined the Nazis and gave it respectability as an aristocrat and successful military officer for the Junkers and industrialists. Other notable members included ex-lieutenant Julius Streicher and Heinrich Himmler, a chicken farmer with strong ideas of social Darwinism.

- On the 8th of November 1923, Hitler declared a "national revolution"; 9 Nov saw a march through Munich, where Hitler had hoped for support from the army and police to take over the city and country. However, shots were fired – four police and sixteen Nazis died; the police, instead, protected the Weimar Republic against the Nazis. The support of police and public opinion was greatly overestimated by the NSDAP, and their tactics were wrong in failing to consider the mechanics of seizing power such as power and phone lines.

Hitler's imprisonment

The trial of the Munich Putsch saw Hitler allowed to stand up and make long, extravagant speeches in the court, which would later be published. The sympathetic judiciary gave him a 9 month sentence in Landsberg Prison. Indeed, while there he was allowed to read books and even write his own – dictating *Mein Kampf* to his deputy Rudolf Hess. The contents outlined his plan for Germany and the world as one of Pan-Germanism, anti-Semitism, anticommunism and removing Versailles in lieu of aggressive foreign policy. He was released in December 1924.

Political outcome of Munich Putsch

- Hitler is a strong man, ruthlessly fighting for the German people and empire that is constrained by the democratic Weimar Republic
- 16 martyrs died for the cause of Nazi ideology
- Nazis gain national exposure, helping lift them from being a minority fringe group

b) Reorganisation and development of NSDAP

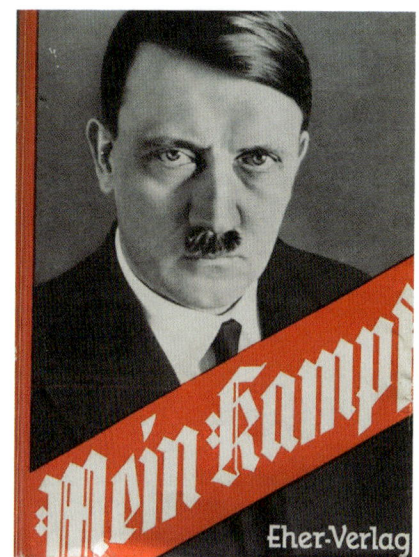

In 1923-4, the NSDAP faced the difficulties of no effective leader, with Hitler in prison after the Munich Putsch, a lack of discipline to organise the extremist beliefs within the group and had descended into power struggles between factions of competing tactics (legalism v Putschs) and ideology (nationalism v socialism). Even when Hitler is released, he is only released on parole and expects 4 more years of sentence; he is not allowed to speak across large parts of Germany until 1927 (with his oratory skills a primary reason for the NSDAP's ascendancy) or enter Prussia. The government's attempt to exile Hitler was rejected by Austria.

In the political sphere, the crisis of hyperinflation had calmed and the policy of 'fulfilment' took place, almost immediately bearing fruit with perceived economic growth under the Dawes Plan. The NSDAP would fail to have a significant impact in a bettering society with such significant internal divisions.

For a while, Hitler deliberately does not interfere in internal divisions in order to later assert his authority and build a cohesive ideology around his cult of personality.

Party reorganisation and Führerprinzip

- Centralisation and bureaucratisation
- Führerprinzip
- Gauleiter regional control
- Legality and SA control
- Hitler Youth

From receiving 6.5% of the vote in May 1924, the NSDAP won just 3% in December elections. Consequently, the Party was re-founded in February 1925. Throughout the year the party was reorganised into a centralised and bureaucratic entity with an index of all members created.

At the party conference in February 1926, a new autocratic and centralised structure was discussed which stressed complete obedience to Hitler and *Führerprinzip*, with adherence to the "Programme of 1920". Regional leaders, *Gauleiter*, were beginning to suggest policies independent of Hitler with Strasser's followers in the north-west beginning to follow a more radical anti-capitalist idea; Hitler consolidated his monopoly of ideology through the formal acceptance of his programme at a membership meeting in May 1926.

Hitler also introduced the policy of 'legality', to fight within the system and law for power. Indeed, as part of this, Hitler attempted to quell the SA and staged a march in July 1926 to indicate party control of its paramilitary arm; from then on the SA would take more mundane roles of military training and stewarding of rallies. In 1926, the Hitler Youth and Nazi Students' Association were founded and ran popular activities for children, with military-style uniforms provided.

Election May 1928 and further reorganisation

Disappointment at the ballot box, only registering around 800,000 votes (2.6%) hence holding only 12 seats in the Reichstag, saw the NSDAP move to further reorganisation. The party consequently created professional bodies in October 1928, with the first as the Association of National Socialist Jurists. More importantly groups were developed to represent specific interests – the most important perhaps being the Agrarpolitischer Apparat (AA) founded in 1930 to draw the peasantry into the movement through propaganda activities.

6. The Rise of the Nazi Party 1929-33

a) Context: Economic and political environment of 1929-33
b) Popular support: Nazi propagandism and electoral successes
c) Role of Elites: Schleicher, von Papen and Hindenburg vs Communism
d) NSDAP: Impact of party organisation and Hitler's personal role
e) Summary table of Hitler's appointment as Chancellor

a) Socioeconomic and political environment of 1929-33

- Economic collapse
    - Wall Street Crash 1929
    - Unemployment and Brüning Austerity

- Autocratisation and Polarisation
    - Use of Article 48
    - Prussian coup d'état
    - Polarisation: Communism and Nazism

Economic collapse

Wall Street Crash 1929

The Wall Street Crash of October saw a massive international depression, and since the Weimar economy was especially dependent on American loans and imports, it saw a massive rise in unemployment as capital was withdrawn that further exacerbated the polarisation of German politics especially after the prior hyperinflation crisis of 1923. Worldwide closures of businesses and bankruptcies dented the growing German industry. Five major banks collapsed in 1931, as the middle classes lost all of their savings. In 1931, the Danatbank collapsed.

Unemployment and Brüning Austerity

33% workers unemployed by 1933; industrial output fell 50% by 1932 as consumer demand drastically decreased. Wages and prices deflated; the economy stagnated and poverty ensued. This economic deflation was catalysed by the policies of austerity pursued by Chancellor Brüning. Following the 1930 election, Brüning found only ⅓ of Reichstag support. Consequentially he dissolved the Reichstag following the SPD condemnation of tax increases. Brüning furthermore reduced unemployment benefits and wages. German exports decreased from 98% of pre-war levels in 1929 to 56% in 1932, with an almost identical decline in industrial production.

The SPD and unions were significantly weakened by unemployment. The psychological effect of economic despair undermined confidence in present structures; the Mittelstand (lower middle class) and peasantry were threatened with a further collapse in living standards. This allowed a route for Nazi propaganda and undermined present structures

Brüning did have one successful policy though, having ended payments on reparations through the Lausanne Conference in 1932 – demonstrating the power of the policy of fulfilment

Autocratisation and Polarisation

Use of Article 48

President Hindenburg made it clear when Brüning became Chancellor (March 1930) that if the Reichstag did not pass the laws he intended, he would rule by decree. This was in the wake of Müller's attempted utilisation of proportional representation through his "grand coalition" government; this was to be the first government based on presidential rather than parliamentary authority. In July 1930, the government was comprehensively defeated on its Finance Bill. The Reichstag rejected attempts to pass the bill by decree by 236-221, but after the President dissolved the Reichstag it was successfully passed by decree. Presidential government was fundamentally established.

As von Papen took the Chancellorship (after Brüning lost Hindenburg's confidence through recommendation by Schleicher), his aim was to establish an authoritarian government in lieu of Weimar democracy; his support was constrained to 68 MPs and ruled with a 'Cabinet of Barons' (no MPs) – this style of government further created a precedent for an autocratic dictator to take the German Chancellorship.

Prussian coup d'état

Authoritarianism as a form of rule was further established through the Prussian coup d'état, in the destruction of the constitutional-democratic system. Political violence in the run up to the election was used as the excuse on 20 July 1932 for the dismissal of the SPD-dominated Prussian government on the grounds it failed to keep the peace. Hindenburg ordered the army to seize control, and he appointed a Reich Commissioner to govern Prussia; the SPD and unions, weakened by unemployment, failed to resist and Prussia had a new authoritarian regime, with a police that followed the orders of Papen and the Reich Commissioner rather than the Weimar state

Polarisation: Communism and Nazism

This economic environment led to polarisation; with the 1931 elections seeing Nazis win 107 seats and 77 for the KPD. However, as later sections will show, the Nazis were able – through a more cohesive movement as established by the Führerprinzip and more sympathy with the elites – to establish this widespread discontent. With a powerful and largely well controlled paramilitary storm troopers unit, they could also use street violence to indicate the strength of Nazism amidst communism that propaganda showed to be playing into the

b) Popular Support: Nazi Propagandism and Electoral Success

- Propaganda

- Electoral successes
    - 1930 – 6.4m
    - July 1932 success – 37%
    - November 1932 waning popularity
    - Nazism as a protest vote

Propaganda

Inextricably linked with increasing electoral success, the appointment of Joseph Goebbels to lead the NSDAP propaganda unit in the spring of 1929 saw the execution of a comprehensive national electioneering programme. Some posters appealed to the need for bread and welfare for the unemployed, others appealed to men looking for work, others appealed to women looking after children amidst Weimar liberalism accused as sexualising young girls; many scapegoated Jews as manipulative capitalists responsible for the plight of the German working class – the posters were deliberately vague with no specific policy details but nevertheless appealed to fears and aspirations across class and gender.

'Saturation' propaganda activities were used by Goebbels with the use of rallies, speeches and lectures – this helped to win large gains in regional areas, for example in Saxony in 1930 where poorer farmers

Electoral successes

Propaganda led to electoral successes for the Nazis.

- The September 1930 election was a triumph for the Nazis; with their Reichstag representation increasing from 12 to 107 seats, capturing 6.4m votes from just 800,000 in 1928. Electoral successes translated to other successes; it weakened the support of the Brüning cabinet, having to rely increasingly on tolerating the SPD and Article 48, and acted as a stimulus to Nazi membership – between September and the end of the year, 100,000 joined up.

- It was 1931 that the real economic collapse hit Germany due to the Hunger Chancellor Brüning's policies. Throughout 1931, the Nazis averaged a stable 40% across local elections.

- The Presidential election of March/April 1932 saw Hindenburg re-elected; despite saturation electioneering Hitler only managed to poll 30% on the first ballot and 37% on the second as opposed to Hindenburg's 50% and 53%. Yet the defeat was still presented as a success since they doubled their vote since the Reichstag election.

The July 1932 electoral success

Elections to the Reichstag in July saw the Nazi percentage of the vote increase to 37% which translated into 230 seats, making it the largest party in the Reichstag. Although not a majority, it helped the NSDAP build further political capital. They had the mandate from the German people to be involved in the government. Indeed, especially since von Schleicher and von Papen could use it against the left as a mass movement with broad support, unique in a multiparty parliament of narrow sectional interest.

November 1932: Waning popularity

In the election of November 1932, after the failure of negotiations between von Papen and Hitler, the Reichstag was dissolved and the elections saw a fall in the Nazi vote of 4 percentage points (to 33%), losing 34 seats. The NSDAP, the largest party, could still vote out any government at will but nevertheless Hitler was appointed as his popularity waned

Who voted Nazi, and why were they popular?

Primarily that of the Mittelstand of civil servants, officials and others damaged by the economic instability of the Republic. The NSDAP failed to attract significant votes from the industrial working class; indeed, the Nazis were weakest in urban areas dominated by the working class – in Berlin (November 1932) the KPD and SPD together gained 54% of the vote. Protestants were typically far more likely to vote NSDAP; but overall, a Nazi vote typically represented a protest vote at the failures of the other parties and the political system itself. A party that aimed to destroy democracy through vague policy was primarily destined to be a protest vote. Nevertheless, the prospect of *Volksgemeinschaft* as a party that transcended class boundaries was unique and hence the only truly nationalist party.

c) Role of Elites: von Schleicher, von Papen and Hindenburg

- Negotiations
    - von Papen's chancellorship
    - von Schleicher's chancellorship
    - Business interest
    - von Papen to control Hitler: "we've hired him"

- Personal motive for Hindenburg

Negotiations

von Papen's chancellorship (June 1932 – Dec 1932)

Brüning, in failing to restore order from political violence, solving the economic crisis, securing Hindenburg's election unopposed and with his deflationary policies angering the army through preventing rearmament, was forced to resign in May 1932.

von Papen not only created the precedent for autocracy through the excessive use of Article 48 and the Prussian coup d'état, but was a personal friend of Hindenburg and a landed aristocrat. He failed to control Hitler: after the July 1932 elections, the Nazi vote reached 37% of the poll – Papen's attempt to enlist Hitler failed when he demanded that he and not Papen had to head the government. Papen was forced to resign – since the NSDAP had the plurality of the Reichstag – as he lacked any support in the country and the army had lost patience with him.

von Schleicher's chancellorship (Dec 1932 - Jan 1933)

Schleicher did no better at restoring order or co-opting the Nazis to give the semblance of popular backing to his policy of creating an authoritarian state. Strasser, the Party's second in command, resigned in frustration at Hitler's refusal to negotiate with Hindenburg and Papen and after Schleicher offered Strasser the Vice-Chancellorship. Without Nazi support, Schleicher's government was not credible – especially strong opposition to his economic policy which was seen as far too conciliatory to the

The November election results, despite the NSDAP's declining vote, indicated the Nazi Party's ability to vote down a government at will and Hindenburg's wish to continue Presidential government through his choice of Chancellor. Nevertheless, the divisions in the party through their evident decline and lack of funds may have been perceived by Hindenburg as a good chance to appoint Hitler Chancellor to manipulate them.

Business input

Despite the fundamental need for Nazi support for any government (best achieved through the appointment of Hitler,) the support of industrialists may have helped convince Hindenburg to von Papen's reconciliation. Indeed, business interests were not particularly fond of Schleicher's  economic policy: they had an obvious preference for authoritarian rule; it was at Kurt von Schröder's house that Hitler and von Papen met in January 1933 – many industrialists wrote to Hindenburg to express support for the NSDAP.

von Papen to control Hitler: "we've hired him"

Moreover, Schleicher, having played a part in the dismissal of von Papen, was outwitted by von Papen who met in secret with Hitler and persuaded Hindenburg to appoint Hitler as Chancellor (and him Vice-Chancellor, with only 3 Nazis including Hitler in the Cabinet) in January 1933. Hindenburg believed that, with a nationalist cabinet to restrain him, the popular support of the NSDAP provided a route of broad support for the peaceful collapse of the Weimar Republic – Hitler's Chancellorship was only intended as a temporary measure.

Personal motive for Hindenburg

In the late 1920s, German agriculture suffered low prices; landowners relied on governments in the east for help – the Osthilfe programme was established. In 1927, Hindenburg had been given back his family's formally bankrupt (Neudeck estate) for his 80th birthday present,  however in 1932 a Reichstag committee investigated the use of Osthilfe funds for gambling and mistresses, implicating Hindenburg's estate. Hitler had promised Hindenburg that the committee would be ended on his Chancellorship.

d) NSDAP: Impact of party organisation and role of Hitler

- NSDAP organisation
    - Propaganda and 'saturation'
    - Centralisation and bureaucratisation
    - Gauleiter regional control
    - Legalism
    - Paramilitary wing of storm troopers
    - Hitler Youth

- Role of Hitler
    - Führerprinzip
    - Rejecting negotiations of vice-Chancellorship

The details of this is are in the section above, but through a strongly hierarchically dominated regional control with absolute obedience to the Führer whose ideology was automatically that of the party, support could be rallied and consolidated within the movement effectively. Through legalism, the means of establishing a dictatorship through popular support and initially within the sphere of the Weimar constitution were actualised. The paramilitary wing of the party were able to violently oppress oppositional communist groups, and the saturation of propaganda reinforced this message.

e) Summary table: Hitler's appointment as Chancellor

Economic and political environment 1929-33	Popular support: Elections and Propaganda	Role of the elites in appointment	Impact of NSDAP organisation and Hitler
Wall Street Crash	Propaganda saturation and targeting (Goebbels)	Role of Papen in negotiations: "we've hired him"	Nazi organisation: • Propaganda • Centralisation • Gauleiter • Legalism • Paramilitary • Hitler Youth
Unemployment and Brüning austerity	1930 breakthrough	Schleicher's failure	
Use of Article 48	July 1932 success	Business input	
Prussian coup d'état	November 1932 waning popularity	Personal motive of Hindenburg	Role of Hitler: • Führerprinzip • Oratory skills • Rejecting negotiations of vice-Chancellorship
Polarisation: Communism and Nazism	Nazism as a protest vote		

Weakness of Weimar democracy can be extrapolated from the three former columns; a combination of bad decisions in the legacy of violence post-WWI and the problems of the Weimar Constitution (Proportional Representation, autocracy, federalism)

Sample questions:

- Why did Hindenburg appoint Hitler as Chancellor in January 1933
- "Hitler's remarkable talents were responsible for his Chancellorship in January 1933". Do you agree with this view?

Controversy: The Nazi Regime

1. Core Content 1933-39

a) Gleichschaltung and consolidation of power
b) Propaganda, and youth
c) Economic Policy
d) Foreign Policy
e) The terror state
f) Volksgemeinschaft
   a. Inclusion: women, working class (success?)
   b. Exclusion: Jews, asocials
g) Opposition (left, religious groups)

a) Gleichschaltung and consolidation of power

Limitations to Hitler's power

- He was appointed Chancellor of the Weimar Republic in a bipartisan Cabinet that included only three Nazis
- He was to be 'controlled' by Vice-Chancellor von Papen
- The most powerful politician continued to be President Hindenburg, with his prestige from his position in the army
- Hitler had to face powerful groups such as the civil service and churches; indeed, also trade unions which the left were powerful in
- The Nazis had popularity on the basis they tackle Germany's economic problems, so now the Nazis would be judged on whether they delivered
- For many in the middle class, the violence and lack of respectability of the Nazis was a major issue; it had to establish broad political consensus

Amongst all this, Hitler was under pressure from his own party; the SA and radicals to implement a full Nazi revolution. Nevertheless, Hitler was able to consolidate power remarkably quickly by the end of 1933 for a number of reasons:

1. There was a widely-perceived threat of Communist seizure
    a. Enabling compliance in the first stage of Gleichschaltung
2. The failure of the left
    a. Misinterpretation of communists
    b. Failure of socialists to organise
3. Nazis gained popularity
    a. March 1933 election
    b. Potsdam Day - respectability
4. Intimidation and manipulation to allow dictatorial governance
    a. Allowed the Enabling Act 1933
    b. Concordat
    c. Gleichschaltung

1. Perceived threat of communist seizure

- In the two elections of 1932, the KPD saw its share of the vote increase from 14.3% In July to 17% in November
- On the streets, the Red Front Fighters' League matched the SA
- The socialists were even stronger; the paramilitary wing (the Reichsbanner) dominated streets across Germany; in November 1932 the SPD received 20% of the vote.

In response to this perceived threat, Hitler told the nation on 10 Feb 1933 that it was his intention to destroy the 'Marxist threat' of both communism and socialism.

The Reichstag Fire

On the night of 27 February 1933, a young Dutchman called Marinus van der Lubbe set fire to the Reichstag as a protest at the repression of the working class. Hitler and the Nazi leadership ignored evidence he had worked alone, and concluded the act was an act of communist backlash. This gave the regime its opportunity to popularly crush communists and use legal means (suspending parts of constitution) to establish power.

Hindenburg supported that Hitler become a dictator to counter the communist threat. Indeed, on 28 February the emergency decree was issued

- Freedom of speech, a free press and freedom of assembly were all suspended; police were given powers to detain suspects without reference to the courts
- Clause 2 allowed the Cabinet to intervene in the government of the states: this power was previously the prerogative of the President

Goebbels ensured that Nazi propaganda portrayed the decree a necessary step in the battle against communism, and it was widely welcomed. Indeed, the decree provided a legal front to the activities of the NSDAP despite undermining the rule of law, with Hitler telling his Cabinet on 28 February that the struggle against communists must not be restrained by "judicial considerations".

The decree was used to justify the arrest, imprisonment and torture of thousands of political opponents – the leader of the KPD Ernst Thälmann was arrested on 3 March and 25,000 political prisoners were in prison in Prussia alone by the end of April.

2. Failure of the left

The failure of the left was in misreading the situation of Hitler's appointment

The Communists believed Hitler's government would not last; as by the doctrines of teleological Marxist historiography, they believed Hitler's appointment as Chancellor signified a crisis in capitalism that would inevitably leave to a proletariat revolution through political and economic collapse. Thus, they did nothing and decided to wait. This allowed the Nazis to launch an assault on the Communists:

- The appointment of 50,000 SA, SS and Stahlhelm (nationalist paramilitary) members as auxiliary policemen on 22 Feb unleashed violence on the left
- On 24 Feb, the police raided and ransacked the head office of the KPD; Goering claimed the evidence discovered in the raid pointed to a communist conspiracy.

The SPD leadership also struggled responding – to use violence would play into the hands of the Nazis, which clearly intended on undermining the socialist movement (having already attempted to close down a number of socialist newspapers). Equally damaging was the split between communist and socialist parties, failing to provide a united front despite together gaining 37% of the popular vote in November 1932.

3. Nazis gained popularity

March 1933 election

With the 28 February emergency decree popular, it paved the way for Nazi electoral success. While their success was not total, the Nazis managed to get 44% of the vote (despite the intimidation of rivals), giving them 288 seats. Even with the 52 seats of their nationalist allies, this was way short of the two-thirds of seats required to alter the constitution. Indeed, after the decree, KPD deputies were banned from the Reichstag (despite gaining 5 million votes), so the result gave Hitler a significant political advantage.

The process of destroying political opposition was to be begun with Himmler setting up the Dachau concentration camp in Bavaria on 22 March to hold political opponents in 'protective custody'

Potsdam Day and respectability

On the opening of the Reichstag in Potsdam on 21 March 1933, Hitler and Goebbels utilised the opportunity for a propaganda triumph. Hitler, wearing morning dress rather than militaristic party uniform, bowed deeply to President Hindenburg and made a very moderate and conservative speech. Many of Germany's respectable and middle classes were reassured. Indeed, this helped acquiesce Hindenburg – the son of Wilhelm II – who witnesses Hitler's commitment to traditional German values; helping Hitler in his aim to undermine the constitution despite not having the 2/3 majority required to alter it.

The same day, Hitler was able to pass the Malicious Practice Law banning criticism of the party and its policies. His intentions were more clear.

4. Intimidation and manipulation to allow dictatorial governance

Enabling Act 1933

On 23 March, Hitler presented the Enabling Act before an intimidated Reichstag, surrounded by brown-shirted SA man. The Act would allow the government the power to pass laws to the cabinet and allowed the government to alter the constitution as it saw fit, and also granted Hitler four years of power as a dictator. The move required 2/3 attendance and 2/3 votes of deputies; with communists barred, the Nazis required the support of the Centre Party (who had 74 seats).

Catholic Church / Centre Party

Many within the Nazi movement saw organised religion to be as much an enemy as the communist or socialist movements; in February there had been a number of attacks against churches and religious figures. The priority for the Catholic Church was to protect its own interests; therefore many Catholics were reassured by Hitler's assurance to the leader of the Centre Party that the Enabling Act would not affect the church and promised he would not restrict Catholic influence in education. The Catholics had no wish to end up as the KPD had, and therefore promised its support – the only party in the Reichstag opposing the bill was the SPD.

Thus the Enabling Act was passed by 444 votes to 94; democracy and the Weimar constitution were at an end.

As part of Gleichschaltung, the Concordat would be agreed on 1 July. As the last party to voluntarily disband on 4 July, they posed the greatest obstacle to the acquisition of absolute power. While Hitler aimed to compromise on its social functions for the time being, his later aim would be to eliminate religious influence - the Catholic Church agreed to give up all of its political activity but their right to congregate and worship in the Nazi state was guaranteed.

Gleichschaltung

- The next step the Nazis took after the Enabling Act was the destruction of local state government; on 31 March all state governments were dissolved by the Minister of the Interior Wilhelm Frick, ordered to reconvene with a majority of Nazis. State governors were appointed with full power to introduce Nazi policies.

- By the Law for the Restoration of the Professional Civil Service of 7 April 1933, Jews and political opponents were thrown out of the civil service.

- On 1 May, the trade unions enjoyed their May Day celebration and the day after, their offices were stormed by the SA – the huge socialist trade union organisation ADGB disbanded and assets seized. On 10 May the German Labour Front (DAF) was established as a unifying Nazi trade union.

- The violence and intimidation led many members of SPD of the socialist SPD to flee abroad, and on 22 June the party was officially banned and its assets seized. Around 3,000 prominent socialists that remained in Germany were arrested and a number killed. Other political parties consequently disbanded.

- On 14 July, the NSDAP was declared the only legal party in Germany

b) Propaganda

Aims of Nazi propaganda

- Goebbels was Reich Minister of Propaganda from 1933-45, and one of Hitler's closest confidants as a vehement anti-Semite

- Goebbels and the Nazis had a low view of the German masses' intellect, and believed propaganda should work invisibly and seamlessly into everyday life to fully indoctrinate people into Nazi ideologies.

- Propaganda was also directed at distinct areas of the population through posters to women and the industrial worker or peasant for example; it was made vague and simple in aims instead of specific policy promises

- Goebbels: "effective propaganda must be reduced to the minimum of essential concepts"; "the most important thing… is to paint your contrasts in black and white"; "make the lie big, make the lie simple, keep saying it and eventually they will believe it"

Forms of propaganda

Press	- Content published rigorously controlled to produce content favourable to the regime; October 1939 a law made editors responsible for 'infringements of government directions' - Nazi ownership of the press from 3% in 1933 to 82% in 1944
Radio	- State regulated since 1925; in 1933 radio stations were taken over by Reich Governors and in April 1934 the Nazis established a unified radio system which Goebbels called the 'spiritual weapon of the totalitarian state' - Transmitted Hitler's key speeches ; workplaces were informed by sirens when these began and attendance was compelled by radio wardens. An audience of 56/70m Germans was estimated in 1935 - 70% of households had sets by 1939, made easier by the People's Radio Receiver – a cheap radio set to increase access to the regime.
Film	- Filmgoers quadrupled from 1933-42, seen as an activity of leisure and relaxation; in 1942, the major film companies were

	nationalised – films were regulated and given funding for political or cultural value. • 1000 films produced, including the famous 'The Eternal Jew' – proved not to be a hit by audiences when many fainted and found Hitler's distorted image of Jews (cockroaches) revolting
Rallies	• Mass rallies strengthened supports' commitment and attracted bystanders to be won over, Goebbels: mass rallies 'transformed people from a small worm to a large dragon'; they were well choreographed, with symmetrical crowds of thousands coordinating in militaristic style to salute the Führer.
Sport	• Sports facilities and activities were organised by Hitler Youth and DAF to be available only for those within those Nazi organisations. With a latent aim of making Germans fit, the sense of community and enjoyment in these facilities was also significant for propagandist purposes. • The 1936 Olympics were a further propaganda success, with the stadium steel and housing obituary memorials to fallen soldiers of WWI and Germany heading the league table – bolstering the social Darwinist rhetoric of Aryanism
Paintings	• Hitler's view of painting became imposed; the modern, reflexive and abstract art of the Weimar period was replaced with clear propagandist visual images, and heroic idealisations of the ordinary German's plight; the biological purity of the Aryan woman and fertile German land reinforced through paintings.
Exhibitions	• These paintings were shown in exhibitions. In 1937, two parallel exhibitions were held in Munich 1) The 'exhibition of great German art', which showed propagandist art in Hitler's vision saw 600,000 attend 2) The 'exhibition of degenerate art', which showed Weimar, 'Bolshevik' and Jewish art saw 2,000,000 attend
Architecture	• Neo-classical and grand architecture, for example the Nuremberg stadium where mass rallies were held in lieu of the modernist Bauhaus degenerate architecture of the Weimar era

Success of propaganda and historiography

- May have built support for the regime and bolstered the Hitler myth, however the propaganda was unlikely to create a strong belief in Nazi ideology

- Hitler became the 'strong man' leader desired by many in Germany, and the paternalistic state with Hitler's cult of personality was polualar, especially when combined with policies of militarisation portrayed in propaganda.

- Hence while there may not have been a strong belief in Nazi ideology, propaganda was significant in creating consent rather than consensus, preventing active resistance against anti-Semitic policies.

- Hughes – the greatest success of Nazi propaganda was that large numbers of Germans became convinced they lived in a Volksgemeinschaft

- Kershaw – Nazi values made little serious dent in traditional class loyalties; Nazi policy failed categorically to break down religious allegiance; the greatest (but only partial) success was on young Germans

Propaganda and Youth

Nazi propaganda was transmitted through youth through two main alleys:

- Hitler Youth
- Education

Hitler Youth

- <u>Aims</u>: to make youth loyal and obedient to Hitler, requiring total obedience to become committed National Socialists. Boys should become strong fighters and girls should bear many children, thus sports activities helped create a youth of physical fitness – competitive sport further reinforced social Darwinism. Finally, the group intended to foster the Nazi ideology in youth, through excitement in the uniformity of group (regardless of class background), anti-Semitism and anti-democracy.
- <u>Methods</u>: activities such as camps, sport and military training were popular. A free Nazi uniform included was also very popular, especially with the parents of working class children. In 1933, all other groups except Catholic Action banned, and in 1936 even this was banned – membership became of social compulsion. Hitler Youth members were encouraged to use violence against weaker children or racial minorities, and standing up to traditional members of authority such as teachers or parents was popular.

- Response of youths: from 108,000 members in 1932 to 6,000,000 in 1936, membership became more widespread and hence included less committed young people; military training became more important in lieu of more popular activities. The more committed Hitler Youths were higher in a hierarchy, with many commanding over their youth peers. To be a member of Hitler Youth was essentially required for any sports or youth activies.

Was Hitler Youth successful?

Yes	No
- Members were taught to obey orders and be exceptionally nationalistic; an immense sense of discipline and patriotism was created in Hitler Youth members - Since no other youth groups were allowed, 90% of parents enrolled their children in the group - Ultimately bolstered the Hitler myth, proclaiming obedience to the Fuhrer and allowing activities only through the Nazi organisation - Partial success, though? Peukert: change over time; war prepration from 1936 saw the militarisation and lessened popularity of Hitler Youth, with increasing absenteeism	- The strictly ideological nature of the Hitler Youth waned as other groups were banned and less committed members joined through coercion or violence of present members, or simply for the sport activities. - This coercion may not indicate true ideological belief and genuine obedience, with one young German having recalled "No one in our class ever read Mein Kampf" - Fischer: it created a "thin ideological veneer" - Sax and Kuntz: "procured a non-resistant yet intellectually inflexible young person, lacking the technical or political skills required for running a modern Nazi empire" - *The development of other groups* Edelweiss Pirates developed in response to the strictly regimented Hitler Youth; they rejected Nazi authoritarianism yet due to military conscription at 17 their nonconformist behaviour tended to be restricted to petty provocations. One of their slogans was, however "Eternal war on Hitler Youth"; numbered 2000 by 1939. Swing Kids centred around swing and jazz lovers in Germany in 1930s; 14-18 year olds (especially middle and upper class); admiring the British and American ways of lives over National Socialism.

Education

- Aims: to encourage the ideology of National Socialism, and create a new generation of leaders for a racially pure Volksgemeinschaft with the wider society taking primacy over the individual.

- Methods: the school curriculum changed; "Heil Hitler" salute was to begin each day, with a curriculum of language, history, geography, chemistry and mathematics militarised for warfare; for example mathematics became the science of war and economics of how much keeping the terminally ill would cost, whereas in history Versailles and the stab in the back myth made up the curriculum. In April 1933, the law for the Restoration of the Civil Service saw about 1200 racially impure or politically 'unreliable' university teachers to be replaced. Many teachers were also sympathetic to Nazism, with 30% having voluntarily joined the party by 1936; by 1937, through coercion, 97% had joined the National Socialists Teachers' League. Schools were no longer co-ed, but separate sex – reinforcing the strict gendered division in Nazi Germany.

- Response of youths: students were forced to join the Nazi-controlled German Students' League, having to score points in sports, yet 25% seem to have avoided this – indicating little genuine interest. Indeed, the schools were not seen as particularly good in terms of education – no Nazi leader sent their child to an "Adolf Hitler" school but instead sent their children to private education.

Similarly to as in Hitler Youth, education created absolute obedience, organisation and discipline but stifled intellectual flexibility and failed to create useful leaders for the future. Students were trained to follow the Fuhrer's will (work towards the Fuhrer – Kershaw), learning speeches off by heart and learning chapters of Mein Kampf rather than genuinely believe or think for themselves.

c) Economic policy

Aims of Nazi economic policy

Elected in the midst of economic catastrophe, the Nazis had to prove they had the capability to deal with the situation to secure their power and popularity; yet they also had to prepare Germany for war and create an Autarky. They faced many problems:

- The Great Depression
- Slump in world trade
- 6 million unemployed
- Lack of natural resources
- Low investment confidence – fear of a trade union state (National *Socialism*)
- Low consumer confidence, fearing unemployment

Economics Minister Schacht was appointed in 1934, and created the New Plan to solve the great depression; he used deficit financing through Mefo Bills, essentially IOUs with interest – the equivalent of a government bond, of which by 1937 12bn RM had been paid out. Banned German imports without permission from the Ministry of Economics, solving the immediate problem but creating problems of food shortages.

Initial Policies

- Public works investments
    - Canals, bridges, rail projects
    - The Autobahn programme – to create the infrastructure for materials transit, creating jobs and a positive international image of efficiency
- Tax concessions
- Subsidies for hiring workers (working class jobs)
- Jobs in government bureaucracy (middle class jobs)

- Some workers pressured to leave job markets (women and Jews), while the Youth Service Register took unemployed young performing manual work such as digging irrigation ditches without pay (neither group appeared in unemployment statistics)

- Trade unions banned as part of Gleichschaltung, replaced by DAF – no more demands for wage increases.

How successful were these policies?

> 1933- unemployment 6 million
>
> 1936- unemployment 1.6 million

The Nazis had *won the battle for work*, and the statistics proved it; propaganda reinforced the message for example through the Autobahn scheme, which has been started under Weimar

Rearmament

After the consolidation of the Nazi state and Gleichschaltung, Hitler in August 1936 gave a rarely direct order in the Four Year Plan Memorandum that "the German armed forces must be operational within four years," and the "German economy must be fit for war in four years". Nevertheless, this still remained relatively vague and required a large degree of 'working towards the Fuhrer" within a polycratic state.

After Schact and the Ministry of Economics warned against rearmament too fast as it would cause inflation. However Goering was a closer associate of Hitler's as a strongly ideological Nazi, and was more optimistic in his approach that would see Germany quickly rearm. Hence, while the Ministry of Economics continued to operate, Hermann Goering was made plenipotentiary of the Four Year Plan.

- Hermann Goering Steelworks

Rival firms forced to invest 130m marks; it was the largest steelworks in Europe and in 1941 had 500,000 workers. The Four Year Plan increased production of key commodities for militarisation such as food and iron and developed ersatz products such as artificial rubber. While distant from outrageously high targets still was successful

(,000 tones)	1933	1942	Target
Steel	19,000	23,000	24,000
Explosives	18	300	323
Oil	1,800	6,300	14,000

However despite massive increases in the *quantity* of these goods, the *quality* was exceptionally low – especially for ersatz products. The drive to work towards the Fuhrer and achieve masses of goods for statistics undermined the actual usability of the products.

Goering attempted to bring about economic self-sufficiency, instead of previous reliance on imports, by encouraging German farmers to produce more food (for example given grants to bring new land under cultivation) and mass producing industrial products. In 1939, Germany was still importing more than a third of its raw material requirements

Tim Mason – Germany forced into war through economic policy

Marxist historiographical approach; focused on how class conflict workers as the momentum of a socially-determined history. Argued Hitler was forced into war because of the failure of the Four Year Plan and the resultant lessened quality of life (food rations, long hours and low pay). Hitler hence goes to war for land, national pride, Volksgemeinschaft and resources to appease the working classes where there was widespread discontent. This likely suggests the Nazi state was inefficient.

How successful was Nazi economic policy 1933-9?

1933-6

Successful	Unsuccessful
Public works programmes For example the Autobahn, house building, road repairs – employed many workers on a short term basis (not important, given military conscription would start soon)	**Unemployment statistics doctored** Jews and women dismissed an did not count as unemployed; nor did the young who were in compulsory unpaid labour – public works programmes made little real dent on unemployment
Rearmament Secretive large orders for military hardware, with Versailles ignored and military spending off public accounts through 'mefo bill' payments	**Quality of life deteriorated** With high taxes, and long hours (despite having a job versus the great depression), quality of life for many Germans deteriorated
"New Deal" Plan Trade deficit left by rearmament requiring huge imports with tariffs making exporters struggle; banned German imports without permission, solving the immediate situation but ultimately creating food shortages.	**Natural recovery** The world economy picked up 1932-3, consumer spending and companies' investment picked up – Hitler was not responsible for the economic recovery in this period
Propaganda success People began to feel pride in rearmament and believed the economic recovery – in thinking the battle for work was won, the Hitler myth was bolstered and Germany gained international prestige	

1936-9

Successful	Unsuccessful
German production increased Steel production increased, for example synthetic rubber very successful Hermann Goering Steelworks were the largest steelworks in Europe with 500,000 workers in 1941 – developed after Ruhr iron and steel companies refused to invest in new furnaces for low grade iron ore in 1937	**Germany not an autarky** Still imported over 1/3 of raw material requirements.
	Poor diets Agricultural production less efficient: workers were drafted into factory jobs and land was given over to airfields. From 1933-9, 1.4m workers left agricultural land; less beer and meat
	Budget deficit massively increased Germany lived beyond its means
	Inefficient, polycratic management Schact v Goering; the former far more experienced but less ideological than the other. No single and comprehensive policy

d) Foreign policy

Aims of Nazi foreign policy

- Fight the perils of Marxism, and the Bolshevik destruction of the German people
- Preserve racial purity and enlarge the German race; overthrow Czechoslovakia and Austria who may flank opposition against the West
- Lebensraum (living space) – for self-sufficiency and Autarky
- Invade Russia, the main enemy – with Bolsheviks and Jews – and annexe the Ukraine as the "bread basket of Europe"
- Ally with Britain; Germany wants a European empire of Central Europe (Mittel Europe) of ethnic Germans, rather than to the Kaiser's African aspirations; Britain, another pure Anglo-Saxon nation, would be unaffected by this.

The army was the most significant opposition to Hitler realising his foreign policy ambitions, being resistant to any policy put forward too quickly. Nevertheless, both the Nazis and the army shared the goal of destroying Versailles and re-establishing Germany as a European empire.

Outline of Nazi foreign policy

Death of Hindenburg	August 1934 – merged the offices of Chancellor and President, War Minister Blomberg issued a new wording of the military which became the "Hitler oath", swearing unconditional obedience to Hitler
1933-5 Early diplomacy	Given the weakness of Germany in 1933, Hitler knew he had to act cautiously; Versailles had severe limitations on the military, the economy was in depression and Germany had no allies. Thus Nazi Germany had to appear acceptable. • Signed a Four Power Pact to revise the Versailles treaty by diplomacy and in 1934 secured a non-aggression pact with Poland to last for 10 years • Intended to distract reaction form Germany's withdrawal from the League of Nations in October 1933, Hitler citing the obvious weakness of the League's failure to secure multi-national disarmament. • Nevertheless, in 1935 Britain, France and Italy signed the Stresa Front which condened German rearmament, reaffirmed the Franco-German border in Versailles, defended Austrian independence (after Hitler threatened to intervene after the assassination of the Austrian Chancellor) and in May France allied with Russia against unprovoked aggression, and Russia promised to defend Czechoslovakia. • Nevertheless, by the end of 1935 rearmament and conscription were successfully introduced as Versailles was directly flouted; Saarland was taken out of LoN control after voting for re-incorporation into Germany; and Hitler secured

	the Anglo-German Naval Agreement in June which permitted Germany to build a fleet of 35% of the strength of the British Navy. • The British, French and Italian alliance crumbled in October 1935 after Mussolini's invasion of Abyssinia, Britain and France condemning the action.
1936 Reoccupation of Rhineland	Exploited the crisis of Mussolini's invasion in March 1936, breaking Versailles by reoccupying the Rhineland with 14,000 lightly armed German troops and 22,000 local police. Hitler instructed troops to retreat come resistance but France could not resist and Germany sympathised with Germany's right to the land.
1937 Blomberg-Fritsch Affair	Blomberg had been War Minister, and before an influential and leading army officer sympathetic to the Nazis; Fritsch was head of the army – both are recorded as having "sharp exchanges" with Hitler over his foreign policy goals. In 1937, Blomberg married a 'woman of the people' who later turned out to be a prostitute, confirmed by Gestapo investigations (some historians have argued Goering encouraged the marriage); the incident was then reported to Hitler by Goering, who was incredibly angry and Blomberg entered voluntary exile. Fritsch was falsely accused of having been the client of a male prostitute; Hitler did not need the embarrassment and accepted the testimony of a rent boy at a concentration camp and dismissed him. Hitler then used the opportunity to appoint himself War Minister, using the opportunity to restructure and remove 12 army generals and 6 from the Luftwaffe.
1938 Anschluss	By 1937, Hitler had re-established German military, diplomatic and economic strength – the army had been increased to 500,000 and key alliances had been formed. The Berlin_Rome Axis confirmed Germany's alliance with Fascist Italy in November 1936, furthered by the Anti-Comintern Pact with Japan. Britain and France appeared inconclusive over their outlook on Germany. Hitler felt it time to make public his expansionist ambitions to his generals from November 1937, to seize Lebensraum. Prohibited by the Treaty of Versailles, a union with Austria was the first stage. Despite deeply divided opinion in Austria, the Austrian Chancellor Schuschnigg was pressured into accepting the union but resisted; an attempted plebiscite failed and Hitler ordered his army to march into Austria. Having entered Vienna on 11 March amidst widespread rejoice, Hitler proclaimed the union of Austria and Nazi Germany.
1938-9 The seizure of Czechoslovakia	Hitler despised the Czechoslovakia as an artificial state of the Versailles settlement; he demanded the incorporation into Germany of the 3.5m German speakers who lived in its northern and western borders (known as Sudetenland), mountainous areas given to the Czech state in 1919 as a protective barrier – fortified by frontier defences and military bases

	Encouraged by Anschluss and claiming discrimination by Czechs, Sudeten Germans agitated in March 1938 for union with the Reich. The Czechs partially mobilised their army, but in September a new rising re-ignited the Sudeten crisis. German intervention in support of Sudeten Germans risked European war, with the state guaranteed by Versailles and Czechs having alliances with Russia and France; British PM Chamberlain addressed the crisis by meeting Hitler in September, and agreed Germany could annex German-speaking provinces who voted by referendum to join the Reich. In a second meeting, Hitler demanded the immediate occupation without a plebiscite; the Czechs consequently mobilised their army. A third meeting saw Britain and France appease Hitler, without the willingness to fight Germany – many in Europe believed it would be Hitler's last territorial demand. This became known as the Munich Agreement, with France, Italy and Britain agreeing but the Czech government not invited. The Sudetenland was seized by Germany in October, and Poland and Hungary each annexed land from the crippled Czech state. In March 1939, Germany invaded the rest of Czechoslovakia without resistance, with the western lands incorporated into the Reich and Slovakia becoming a puppet state.
1939 Conquest of Poland	In response to the clarity after Hitler's invasion of Czechoslovakia in March 1939 as the Germans embarking on a policy of eastward expansionism, Britain and France guaranteed the independence of Poland on 31 March. 1. Hitler tried to reinforce his alliance with Italy by the 'Pact of Steel' on 22 May 1939 2. Foreign Secretary Ribbentrop and the Russian Foreign Minister Molotov secured a Nazi-Soviet pact on 23 August, whereby Germany and Russia agreed to partition Poland and not attack each other for at least two years, allowing Hitler to seize half of Poland without fighting a war on two fronts 3. On 28 August, Hitler demanded the return of lands to Poland lost by Versailles, claiming Poles were persecuting German speakers. Germany invaded Poland 1st September. 4. Britain declared that Germany withdraw, and after this was ignored declared war on 3 September. Hitler unleashed rapidly advancing infantry and support units, devastating Poland's old-fashioned cavalry army. While Russia attacked in the east, Britain and France could do nothing to save Poland and Poland surrendered on the 27th of September 1939.

| | Foreign policy ||
	Strong dictator / efficiency	Weak dictator / inefficiency
Rhineland militarisation	Quickened pace toward European domination and conquest at will of the Fuhrer; Britain did not see it necessary to intervene and France had slashed defence spending; consolidated Hitler's dictatorship through popularity – perceived as a man of action	Told troops to withdraw upon any sighted opposition by Allied forces; 14,000 lightly armed troops and 22,000 local police.
Blomberg-Fritsch	Classic example of Goering "working towards the Fuhrer" Hitler in the end gained absolute control of the military	Kershaw: the crisis was accidental, but Hitler took the opportunity to establish control of the army as an opportunist dictator.
Early diplomacy and rearmament	Four Power Pact to revise the Versailles treaty by diplomacy and in 1934 secured a non-aggression pact with Poland to last for 10 years – dictator skills strengthened through diplomacy By the end of 1935 rearmament and conscription introduced as Versailles flouted; Saarland was taken out of LoN control	Hitler had to act within constraints of the Stresa Front in 1935 and the May Franco/Russian alliance Anglo-German Naval Agreement in June 1935 only technically permitted Germany to build a fleet of 35% of the strength of the British Navy. Only possible due to the respective positions of France and Britain
Anschluss	Effectively Hitler had his way despite the prohibitions of Versailles. Effectively overrode Austrian Chancellor's request for a plebiscite, undermining their sovereignty and indicating the military strength of Hitler's Germany.	Based on the consent and support of the German and many Austrian people. Indeed, it was not instant and was pushed forward Goering who was interested in Austria's raw materials for his steelworks and Four Year Plan, and it was his telephone call with the Austrian chancellor that saw the surrender of Austria.
Seizure of Czechoslovakia	Was able to take Czechoslovakia effectively through manipulating foreign leaders and through a strong military force undermining that of the Czechs; manipulating Chamberlain by at first accepting a plebiscite but then rejecting it.	Ultimately required the acquiescence of British, Italian and French forces in order to act – not necessarily a master dictator, and still evidently constrained by Allied forces. Perhaps also an opportunist dictator – only acting within the scope of crisis.

Conquest of Poland	Engineering of alliance with Italy and Russia	International forces now more important – Britain declared war;
	Effectively defeated Poland and took a good deal of its land, merely through Hitler's decision to do so – a master dictator	Poland not a strong military force – surrendering in less than a month; Hitler could not command the support of Britain and France and entered into a war he did not want to
		He was fighting with Russia against another Germanic Anglo-Saxon ethnically pure nation Britain, and too early to have gained the military strength desired

Historiography: relationship between economic and foreign policy

Inefficient, weak dictator

Mason – economic discontent among the working class forced Hitler to go to war

Tooze and Steiner – economic problems forced Hitler to go to war to pay back mefo bills.

Efficient, strong dictator

Overy – Hitler only wanted a localised war with Poland, and a peace deal with the USSR before invading them. He contends Mason's conclusion, citing a "low incidence of social unrest" – Hitler is essentially a strong dictator, going to war because it was part of his planned foreign policy.

e) The terror state

a) Was Hitler's dictatorship based on consent or consensus?
b) Was Hitler's Germany a master or a weak dictatorship?

1. *The Gestapo, SS, SA and the police state*
2. *The Night of the Long Knives*
3. *Euthanasia and T4 Axiom*

	1. Gestapo, SS, SA and the police state	
	Evidence of consensus	Counter-evidence of consensus
Historiography	Gellately: "self-surveillance society" While people mainly informed for selfish reasons, there was a significant amount of informing based on genuine support for rooting out the 'bad' elements of society, citing that in Würzburg there were 21 Gestapo agents for 1 million people. A desire for strong government, reaffirmed through terror, won more support than it lost; coercion led to 'consent'. Johnson: "targeted terror" The Nazis and the German population formed a grim 'pact', with normal Germans turning a blind eye to Gestapo persecution and the Gestapo in turn overlooking minor offences by ordinary Germans. Terror was targeted on opponents: Jews, Communists, gypsies, the disabled, homosexuals, Jahovas Witnesses and beggars. For example in 1933 Beggars Week saw 100,000 beggars 'disappeared' and swept off the streets to much popular acclaim; terror among most was popular, including Night of the Long Knives.	Evans: "all-pervasive terror state" It was the Gestapo among other agencies that kept Germans under surveillance rather than Germans themselves in a 'wider net of terror' including the SS, SA, doctors, tax inspectors, state and party police, social workers, employers and teachers brought together in Gleichschaltung. The element of top-down terror should not be underestimated, with "fear and terror integral parts of the Nazi armoury of political weapons" from the start, with a "social and cultural milieu" engaged in the terror state. Mallman & Paul: Gestapo limitations Gestapo policing was based on denunciations, but the terror state was manipulated by the population for their own benefit. For example, petty feuds over property, neighbours who did not get along or individuals engaged in arguments could be denounced. The extent of the use of terror and repression makes the idea of a consensus state difficult to believe.
Evidence	In Saarbrücken, 88% of cases of 'slander against the regime' were a result of denunciations, while 8% were as a result of the activities of the Gestapo.	In Saarbrücken, in 1939 there were only 50 Gestapo informers.

Master dictator	Weak dictator
Effective all-pervasive terror state effectively actualising the Fuhrer's will Himmler effectively controlled all effective police forces in the SS-Gestapo complex, often referred to as a 'state within a state'. In 1936, Himmler – Hitler's close confidant - was appointed head of all German police, having been head of the SS from 1929 and then the Gestapo from 1933; the NHSA was created to draw together state and party police in 1939. Huge extent of repression: - 1942: 30,000 Gestapo officers - 1939: 50,000 SD officers - 1933-45: 800k detained for resistance - 1939 – 163,000 in Gestapo 'protective custody' Hitler reined in the polycracy of running both the SA and the SS, and the SS-Gestapo complex was ultimately prevailing after Hitler undermined the SA forces against him through: - Night of the Long Knives – Rohm and SA leaders killed; SS became main police arm of the Nazi Party - Ending SA military activity May 1934 - Himmler as leader of the SS was dedicated to actualising the Fuhrer's will and would later become the architect of the holocaust through the SS	Polycratic police state based on the manipulation of Himmler Many different police forces: Orpa (municipal police), Sipo (security police, umbrella for Gestapo [secret state police] and Kripo [criminal police] – run by Heydrich), SD (security service, umbrella for foreign and domestic intelligence – run by Heydrich) Ernst Röhm as head of the SA had argued in June 1933 a National Socialist Revolution would occur regardless of its support from the establishment or lack thereof; this was a direct to Hitler's political authority, however Röhm was brought into the Cabinet by the end of the year. The SA for a while acted as a law unto itself; it has its own police force (Feldjäger), which acted independently of the Gestapo; by 1934 the SA numbered 2.5million members; in Feb 1934, Röhm demanded he be able to take over national defence but Hitler disallowed this, choosing to supported the armed service over the storm troopers. The SA was also in competition with the SS (and Heydrich and Himmler) to be the most powerful Nazi organisation in the feudal competition – this relied on the destruction of the SA. Rohm held contempt for the party organisation, and SA excesses in Prussia upset the regional governor Goering; it was in all other interests that in May 1934, Hitler suspended SA military exercises.

2. The Night of the Long Knives (Op Hummingbird) (30 June 1934)

- Directed primarily at SA leadership but also some conservatives were targeted, ensuring there would not be attempt to block him succeeding Hindenburg
- Across the country as many as 200 people were murdered including, Röhm, von Schleicher, von Bose (author of Marburg speech) and Strasser on the left of the Nazi Party
- On 3 July the state made its own actions legal; the only Catholic left in the Cabinet signed the law as did all other Cabinet colleagues. A purge of Röhm's supporters followed.

	Master dictator	Weak dictator
Historiography	**Removing Röhm's challenge to his authority** - In Feb 1934, Röhm demanded he be able to take over national defence and had previously made comments of how a National Socialist Revolution would occur with or without the support of the establishment, the SA a huge power and was further to the left of the Nazi party - Röhm was a homosexual **Removing von Papen's crippling vice Chancellorship** - 17 June 1934, von Papen criticised cults of personalities and dictatorship at the Marburg Speech, and further criticised Nazi violence and continuous revolution - The speech was written by Young, a famous conservative **Could justify murder through propaganda** - Population under impression Hitler had prevented a revolution; seen as purifying – any excesses were blamed on those other than the Führer - Need for strong man post Weimar; support of Hindenburg and the army - Fear of crtiicising the regime **Consolidated support of army** - Through removing the threat of the SA and using the army to purge it brought the army closer to the regime - After Hindenbrug's death on 2 August, the army would then swear unconditional obedience to the Führer, rather than the constitution.	**Manipulated by other key Nazis** - Himmler, Hess and Goering fed Hitler incorrect rumours about an SA plot with Röhm planning to overthrow Hitler - Himmler's SS spread this message, while Goering saw his Gestapo spy on the SA and creates false intelligence - Part of the "feudal competition", with other Nazis looking to increase their own power **The final trigger** - Hitler visited Hindenburg at his Neudeck estate, with General Blomberg also happening to be visiting. - He gave Hitler an ultimatum to rid of the SA or the army would get rid of Hitler; Hitler required the support of the elites who still had vested power more than the SA, but ultimately was not left with the choice.

	3. Targeted terror: Euthanasia (Aktion T4)	
	Master dictator	Weak dictator
	Programme begun by Hitler Hitler single handedly began the programme of mass extermination of disabled individuals, within months of receiving the letter; soon this was not only to be babies but older children as well.	**Access to the mailroom** Polycracy: Philipp Bouhler won access to the mailroom, with mostly trivial letters and from persecuted individuals; picked those that he believed would fulfil Hitler's will in "working towards the Führer". It was him rather than Hitler that picked the 1938 letter from a father asking to kill his mentally disabled child.
	Consensus dictatorship	Coerced terror state
	A system of whether children should die was based on the opinions o 3 medical professionals in a questionnaire from the Reich Health Ministry. Without being given extra orders, doctors stopped filling in forms by 1940 and instead selected children they wanted to kill, blaming this on diseases. In doing so, they believed they were working towards the Führer in a system of **cumulative radicalisation** based on consensus of state institutionalised social Darwinism; Hitler gave the vision of pure race, but doctors' policy is extrapolated from this. It soon expanded to adults and the elderly too.	In August 1941, Catholic Cardinal von Galen spoke against the euthanasia as "life unworthy of life", criticising the principle of deciding when people should die. Later in the month, Hitler suspended the programme which had accounted for over 100,000 deaths by this point – seeing it would cause widespread unpopularity across Catholic communities. The Cardinal was left unharmed, to avoid making him a martyr, but three parish priests who distributed the sermon were beheaded. Regardless of popular opinion, the Nazi euthanasia program quietly continued, but without the widespread gassings. Drugs and starvation were used instead and doctors were encouraged to decide in favour of death whenever euthanasia was being considered.

f) Volksgemeinschaft

i) Inclusion in the Volksgemeinschaft

Working class: state paternalism

1. Strength through Joy (KdF)

As part of Gleichschaltung, trade union offices were ransacked on 2 May 1933, with over the next few days 169 trade unions placed under Nazi control. They were replaced by the DAF (German Labour Front) on 10 May, whose membership grew from 5m in 1933 to 22m in 1939

The DAF was run by "Reich drunkard" Robert Lay, whose objective was to spread Nazi propaganda in the workplace and win the support of workers through material improvement and state welfare. More personally, he worked within the feudal competition and would want to create a labour empire, immediately putting him in a position of hostility with Hermann Goering (who would nevertheless win with his close proximity to Hitler)

From November 1933, the "Strength through Joy" programme was introduced. The idea was of collective work producing benefits for the workers, through luxuries previously unavailable such as cars, holidays, museum and concert visits.

- November 1933: Beauty of Labour, a subdivision of KdF, improved conditions and facilities in factories – improving lighting, ventilation, cleanliness, better work canteens. Ley called it a "major blow against the class system"

- Holidays, cheap hotels and bed and breakfasts; break from overcrowded industrial cities to the German countryside. By 1938, 180,000 workers had been on a KdF cruise and 10m (1/3 of the workforce) went on a state-financed holiday.

- Cheap rail fares; communication with other Germans in a Volksgemeinschaft

- Cars; travel around Germany. From 1938, workers were encouraged to save towards a Volkswagen (People's Car); workers had the opportunity to save 5 marks a week into a fund, eventually allowing them to receive a car. However as the war came, the funds and factories shifted toward the war effort and no worker received a car.

2. Winterhilfe

"Winter help" organised annual collections and offered charity to the unemployed and destitute. Contributions increased from 350m RM 1933-4 to over 900m RM 1940-1.

3. One-Pot Meals

Winterhilfe was in part funded by contributions to take part in "one pot" meals – communal meals in which bankers and workers were seen eating traditional rural dishes such as casseroles together

---

Failures of eroding class boundaries

KdF
- The "Beauty of Labour" programme was primarily woman decorating workplaces; through the 1936 four year rearmament plan, work hours would be increased and the work would become more intense – cosmetic changes did little to change the fact people were overworked and underpaid, while capitalist classes profited from the industrialisation
- The KdF scheme was deeply unpopular with the middle classes, and many hotel owners withdrew from the scheme when they had rowdy working class guests

Winterhilfe
- The increasing expenditure of Winterhilfe may indicate that class divisions were not eradicated, but rather grew during the era of the Third Reich.

One pot meals
- While the one-pot meals were potentially popular with the working classes, they were unlikely to have been ideologically persuasive, and even less so to have made people Nazis. Indeed, while propaganda showed Nazis and bankers to eat together, in reality this was not the case – it just provided the *illusion* and sense of a Volksgemeinschaft.

In reality, workers real incomes were depressed by Winterhilfe and DAF membership; 18% deductions from the state in the Third Reich versus 15% in Weimar.

Overall the working classes were subject to a propaganda success in Volksgemeinschaft rather than an actual one.

Women

Policies and Nazi attitudes toward women were based on both using women as a tool to achieve Aryan racial purity through their childbearing function, and keeping them within the sphere of domestic work and childrearing in line with traditional values – a far cry from the liberation of the Weimar era. Often, these two objectives provided de facto contradictions and confusions in policy.

- Conservative and socially traditional women did support the Nazi party, despite their open intentions to reverse the suffrage and political roles of women in the Weimar period – national stability was deemed of greater concern

- Alfred Rosenberg – a major Nazi theorist – hypothesised that soon women would be of no concern in political life since their primary role was the propagation of the Master Race.

- In some ways the Nazis were consistent: Hitler kept Eva Braun out of sight, while Goebbels' wife Magda played only a very discrete role. The SS journal frowned upon use of jewellery, lipstick, perfume and high-heeled shoes. Nevertheless, this was contradicted by Goebbels' affair with the racially inferior Czech film star Lída Baarová. Even Eva Braun had habits Hitler disapproved of, including sunbathing naked, smoking and wearing makeup.

Policy of traditionalism & childbearing	Contradictions
- The 1933 Law for the Encouragement of Marriage provided a loan of 1000 RM for newlyweds; it decreased with each born child, becoming a gift upon the fourth child. - Concerns about a falling birth rate became more intense, with in 1938 childlessness was made a suitable ground for divorce - In 1938 the Mother Cross medal was established to reward those with large families; bronze for four children, silver for six and gold for eight children. The rewards excluded those as 'genetically unfit' or with children from several partners – these awards were given annually on 12 August, the birthday of Hitler's mother and on 10 May – Mother's Day. - In 1934, all married women doctors and civil servants were dismissed and from 1936, no women could act as a judge. - Several million German women had visited the new Maternity Schools to train them to be mothers; indeed, the infant mortality rate was halved in Himmler's Lebensborn maternity homes from 1935 - Marriages increased from 516k 1932 to 740k 1934 (but due to economic optimism?)	- The drive for an increased birth rate was seen as more important than legitimate children; as such: - The Lebensborn programme deterred abortion amongst women who became pregnant from outside of marriage - From 1938, the relaxation of divorce laws allowed remarriage with the possibility of children - While abortion and contraception had been banned, many women underwent abortions accompanied by forced sterilisation on the grounds of racial hygiene - The actual number of women in the workplace actually rose in real terms from 36% in 1933 to 37% in 1939; with the inclusion of annexed territories, this became 50% - driven by the expansion of armament industries. Indeed, in 1939 almost a quarter of employed women had children after in October 1937 the demand was ended that a woman leave her job before receiving the marriage loan. - Nazi propaganda depicted German woman in simple peasant clothing, but nevertheless most female consumers preferred French brands and followed sewing patterns in *Vogue* – this has been termed by Broszat as *Resistenz*

Youth: as aforementioned

ii) Exclusion in the Volksgemeinschaft

Asocials

Group	Why were they excluded?	How were they treated by the regime?
The mentally ill and the disabled	Since the Nazis focuses on race in a Volksgemeinschaft, unhealthy genes would weaken the race.	Forced compulsory sterilisation of the hereditarily ill, to prevent the genes passing on to children. In the years 1933-45 about 350,000 people were sterilised; by 1939 the policy developed into euthanasia after a father sent Hitler a letter requesting his deformed son be 'put to sleep' (typical of the random policy decisions made in Third Reich). A special unit – T4 – was established to kill disabled children; the government registered disabled children and records were examined by doctors who determined whether they would die; by 1944 200,000 people deemed mentally/physically disabled had been killed by starvation, lethal injection or gas.
Asocials	A very broad term for those who did not fit into the Volksgemeinschaft; in 1938 defined as vagabonds, gypsies, beggars, prostitutes, alcoholics, eccentrics and juvenile delinquents. Most obvious manifestation of asocial behaviour was unwillingness to work	In 1933, there was a round-up of half a million vagrants, divided into the orderly who were given work and the disorderly who were imprisoned in camps. As unemployment declined, pressure on those not working grew and thousands were sent to concentration camps where many died. The Nazis increasingly justified this policies through stressing the biological origins of asocial behaviour.
Homosexuals	Another group deemed to be asocial – not only did homosexual behaviour deeply offend the traditional moralities of Nazis but was also believed to work against the laws of nature and Germany's population growth	In 1936 the Reich Central Office for the Combatting of Homosexuality and Abortion was established – Himmler tried to establish a register of homosexuals, especially concerned by the level of homosexuality in the SS. In 1937 he ordered that homosexual SS officers should be sent to concentration camps; eventually between 10,000 and 15,000 homosexuals were arrested and sent to camps – some were castrated and became the object of medical experiments. Lesbians were not subject to formal prosecution as they were not seen as a threat to the nation.
Members of religious sects	Although cautious about dealing with Christian churches, the atheistic and Darwinist, reducing human life to biological determinism, acted fiercely against minority sects – especially Jehovah's Witnesses who had refused to join the army and swear allegiance	Whole families of Jehovah's Witnesses were arrested, and about one third of Germany's population of JWs died in concentration camps; other groups such as Christian Scientists and Seventh Day Adventists.
Gypsies	Were not initially hostile to gypsies, but with their distinctive appearance and lifestyle had long been subjects of suspicion – the radicalisation that followed in 1930s saw them become general victims,	In 1938, Himmler issues a 'decree for the Struggle against the Gypsy Plague"; in 1939 they were sent to camps before being expelled to Poland. In December 1942 Himmler ordered their transferral to Auschwitz, where there was a special gypsy camp – 11,000/20,000 of those sent there were gassed. As German control extended through Europe, more gypsies became victims and it is estimated half a million gypsies were killed.

Jews and the development of Anti-Semitism

In 1933, 0.7% of Germany's population was Jewish – this was declining. Primarily employed in medicine, law and teaching rather than capitalist industries, Jews were very well integrated into German society, with the leading Jewish organisation of the 20th century called the "Union of German Citizens of Jewish Faith". Indeed, contrary to the "stab in the back" myth, 20% of German Jews fought for Germany in WWI – the most represented of all ethnic groups.

Very little anti-Semitism was felt in Germany prior to 1933, save some elements of conservative groups. Hitler's *Mein Kampf* discussed how he had encountered Jews at school whom he considered untrustworthy, and in Vienna found that Jewish people looked unusual and not German, prompting him to buy "some anti-Semitic pamphlets for a few Heller (pence)". Anti-Semitism had grown more respectable post WWI in Germany. Nevertheless, Nazi policy was based on distortion and misrepresentation of Jews for no particularly rational reason – the ineptly named "final solution" not particularly solving any problem other than those manufactured by the NSDAP.

Jews were portrayed as hidden, sneaky and shape shifting powerful figures exploiting the pure Aryan master race for their personal material and sexual gain. Russia's significant Jewish population gave rise to the link between Jews and Bolshevism, involved in a conspiracy for world domination – Lenin's Red Terror just the beginning. The German woman was powerless to the manipulative Jew, who was represented in medical professions such as gynaecology with a sexual grotesque and as a paedophile praying on German children, without the hero of Adolf Hitler who had risen from the acquiescence to this horror of the Weimar Republic to solve Germany of its Jewish problem and reaffirm the Aryan master race as dominant across Europe in its ethnically pure Volksgemeinschaft. The Jews effectively provided the Nazis with a scapegoat, with a small and self-contained population, to load on any of Germany's economic or military problems of their choosing.

The powerful fear mongering propaganda success propelled by Goebbels' machine was successful, but there was never universal hatred for Germany's Jewish population, nor were the Nazis successful in mobilising much passionate support.

1933 Jewish boycott

After Hitler came to power in January 1933, an international boycott on German goods followed. To retaliate, on the 1st of April 1933 the Nazi boycott of Jewish shops followed. The Nazi rank-and-file demanded action, forcing Hitler to act. Schacht told Hitller it was a poor economic policy, with a lapse in American investment and less economic activity detrimental, and Hitler was forced to back down – the boycott lasting only one day. In Berlin alone, there were 50,000 Jewish owned businesses. Despite SA intimidation outside Jewish stores, with Stars of David painted on windows, the boycott was ignored by many Germans who continued to shop in Jewish-owned stores.

A week later, on 7 April 1933, the Law for the Restoration of the Professional Civil Service was passed, which restricted employment in the civil service to "Aryans." This meant that Jews could not serve as teachers, professors, judges, or other government positions. Jewish government workers, including teachers in public schools and universities, were fired. Doctors followed closely behind. Jews were barred from claiming any rights as war-veterans (35,000 German Jews died in the First World War).

1935 Nuremberg Laws

The summer of 1935 had been marked by an escalation of anti-Semitic violence; the perpetrators were Nazi activists voicing frustration with two years of Nazi power yet still no significant action on the 'problem' of the Jews. Young members of the SA, disoriented by the Night of the Long Knives in 1934, found an outlet in anti-Semitic hooliganism. By August the disorder became out of hand, and Schacht was once again concerned about economic damage – on the 8th of August, Hitler ordered mass indiscriminate anti-Semitic action must stop, and it did so instantly.

Nevertheless Hitler was aware of the grassroots demand for action. Hitler announced laws at the party conference at Nuremberg in September; the passing of the law was rushed, with no definition of who was or was not Jewish. The laws banned marriage and sexual relations between Jews and gentiles; the laws were effectively opportunistic legislative improvisation, and indicated Hitler's weakness as a dictator in having to respond to party action. However, in the opposite sense, they reflected the realisation of his anti-Semitic ideological vision and opportunism did not necessarily indicate a lack of efficiency as a dictator.

Kershaw has argued the Nuremberg Laws "had been a compromise adopted by Hitler, counter to his instincts, to defuse the anti-Jewish agitation in the country, which over the summer had become unpopular". While many Germans had been appalled by the violence of the summer, they nevertheless accepted the laws.

From 1933-5, Hitler played a leading role in the formulation of anti-Semitic policy but Nazi party activists in "working towards the Führer" initiated the unrest on initiative, to which Hitler responded because it suited his own goals – nevertheless, he determined how far anti-Semitic actions went.

1938 Reichkristallnacht

On 9-10 November there was an anti-Semitic pogrom in Germany; over 100 synagogues destroyed, 8,000 shops of Jews vandalised, over 100 Jews murdered and 30,000 Jewish men taking into concentration camps. The event pre-empted 80,000 Jews leaving Germany. Local leaders coordinated the violence.

The pogrom was a response to the assassination of a German diplomat in Paris on 8 Nov. This coincided with the 15th anniversary of the Munich Putsch, with all of the Nazi hierarchy gathered in Munich. The event came after developing anti-Semitism, with brutal treatment of Vienna Jews in March after Anschluss; from October all Jews required a 'J' stamp in their passports.

In 1939 the Nazi Supreme Court investigated the pogrom looking for evidence of 'criminal behaviour'. Its severest action was sentencing two party members to be banned from holding office in the party for three years for raping a Jewish woman, not for the crime of rape but for "race defilement".

Many Germans anti-Semitic yet few sharing Hitler's homicidal anti-Semitism – there is significant historiographical debate about the public reaction to the event.

- Peukert – 'almost unanimous public obloquy and indignation'
- Goldhagen – Germans 'let the authorities know that they concurred in the unfolding eliminationist enterprise'
- Friedlander: 'the majority of Germans accepted the steps taken by the regime and looked the other way
- Ultimately very difficult to show opposition in the totalitarian police state of Nazi Germany; while many may have been opposed, they took care not to show it.
- The young were the most supportive of the program, but Nazi propaganda was not wholly successful since the majority of Germans opposed the pogrom – despite the regime's representation of Crystal Night as spontaneous anger.

Reichkristellnacht and Hitler's efficiency

Hitler ordered Goebbels to let the demonstrations go on, withdraw the police and see that "the Jews must fell the people's fury". The Nazi Supreme Court found that on the 10th of November, Goebbels had notified officials that Hitler believed the party should not organise demonstrations but not oppose them where they arose spontaneously – all party officials understood this to mean that the party should not appear (with officers in uniform) as the originator but in reality should carry them out. This is evidence the party worked by decoding implicit messages easily decipherable by the party faithful. Goebbels found favour through Reichkristallnacht after his affair with a Czech woman, working within the feudal competition – the best way to appeal to the Führer had been anti-Semitism.

Nevertheless, because these messages were implicit, Hitler could distance himself from what had taken place and hence any criticism – which came from foreign press and those concerned with the massive damage to the German economy. This did not however translate to specific policy dictatorship – rather, it is evidence Hitler's macro control over the vision and direction of policy at all levels was absolute. Kershaw argues this was part of cumulative radicalisation and spelled the path to genocide, to fully realise Hitler's ideological vision.

1939: Hitler's prophesy

Hitler declared that he "wanted to be a prophet again" on the Jewish question and noted: "if international finance Jewry within Europe and abroad… should once more succeed in plunging the peoples into world war… then the consequence will not be […] a victory of Jewry, but on the contrary… the destruction of the Jewish race in Europe". Whether this was a vision, plan or just random sentiment for a "final solution" has been questioned. Nevertheless, the violence of the rhetoric indicates Hitler's comfort towards the later peacetime Nazi years in openly alluding to genocidal anti-Semitism.

g) Opposition to the regime 1933-39

Types of opposition

- Passive resistance
- Protest
- Non-conformity
- Civil disobedience

Group		Effective opposition	Ineffective opposition
Church		Their aim was to defend the church rather than weaken the regime itself; nevertheless self-defence was an obstacle to a total totalitarian state since much religion – especially Catholicism – was incompatible with Nazism.	
	Catholics	In March 1937, Pope Pius saw a encyclical on the Nazi regime smuggled into Germany and read in all Catholic churches, undermining the Concordat between the Reich and the Holy See; 300,000 copies were distributed. In November 1936, the Oldenburg Nazis removed crucifixes from schools. Bishop Galen protested, which led to a public demonstration, and the cancellation of the order.[On 11 November 1938, following Kristallnacht, Pope Pius XI joined Western leaders in condemning the pogrom.	Hitler had undermined political Catholicism through the Concordat in 1933, which meant the Centre Party had little of a body to voice their concern. Catholic schools, youth groups (from 1936) and newspapers were closed, and a propaganda campaign against the Catholics was launched. Significant support for the regime in congregations of middle class women: opposition to homosexuality, abortion and Judaism popular policies – traditional gender roles. Many leading Catholics were killed in the 1934 Night of the Long Knives. After Pius' encyclical, Gestapo raided the churches the next day to confiscate all the copies they could find, and the presses that had printed the letter were closed. Staged prosecutions of Church clergy followed. By 1939, the Catholic Church was keen to stress its patriotism during the war and recognising the strength of the regime needed to compromise for its own protection

	Protestants 2/3 of German population	Gestapo reports commented that given Hitler's refusal to back German Christians with any force (himself a social Darwinist, sceptical of religious belief), the attempted synthesis of German Protestantism and Nazism through the Reich Church had failed, with Churchgoers in rural area resenting the substitution of traditional rituals for Nazi endorsed ones. Some pastors in the Confessional Church were critical of the Nazi regime, one Franconian pastor in his Sunday Mormon declaring "a proper Christian cannot be a National Socialist at the same time".	German Evangelical Church an extremely conservative institution; strongly nationalist, having presented WWI as a religious crusade against Catholics in France and Belgium, and Orthodoxy in Russia. Thus saw communism, socialism and Jewry as enemies of their faith and state; Hitler shaking Hindenburg's hand in the Garrison Church (the burial site of Prussian kings) symbolised the legitimisation of Nazism for many protestants. By June 1933, the Evangelical Church was centralised into a "Reich Church". By 1937, over 700 pastors of the Congressional church had been imprisoned, with Protestant churches too divided to offer real opposition, with many fearing the Left more than Nazism. With the rise of Adolf Hitler schools, from 84% of children attending denominational schools in 1934, by 1937 this had fallen to 5% in Munich. The church was effectively driven from public life.
Left		There were nevertheless an estimated 400 strikes between 1933 to 1935, with many workers maintaining links with illegal political parties. Violence was often used – indeed, Overy has identified 'no go' areas for Nazi officials in some working class districts of industrial cities. The SPD in exile was based in Prague and organised underground groups such as the Berlin Red Patrol and the Hanover Socialist Front, distributing leaflets. The KPD also formed underground cells - even in the DAF; the Rote	No legal organisations that could be used for opposition and direct action. All parties except the NSDAP were banned in July 1933, and a wave of arrests hit their leaders. Two thirds of members of KPD underground cells were arrested; the action of illegal political parties was ultimately hugely restrained and required absolute impassioned commitment given the massive Nazi terror apparatus. Indeed, terror increased throughout the period – in 1933, 64 communists were sentenced to capital punishment, becoming 117 by 1938.

	Kapelle (Red Orchestra) spy organisation sent information to the USSR. Nevertheless, they had a clear alternative ideology (unique among oppositional groups) and international support from the USSR.	
Youth	Failure of Hitler Youth, development of other groups: Edelweiss Pirates and Swing Kids	Success of Hitler Youth (aforementioned) Youth opposition very seriously by the regime, with Himmler organising public executions – would be detrimental to the Tausendjähriges (thousand year) Reich – made these groups comparatively small, with Edelweiss 2000 members by 1939.
Conservatives	Initially major critics in the government; for example in June 1934 Papen pleaded in a speech for greater freedom, and in August 1935 Schacht deplored anti-Semitic violence; some government officials planned an alternative government. Traditional elites, especially in the Kreisau Circle at von Moltke's estate - a small group of officers and professionals who had come together to oppose Hitler. Consisted of old Prussian military elites, who had the support of the army.	Decreased over time through Gleichschaltung and the consolidation of the regime, especially through miraculous foreign policy successes provoking nationalism lost in WWI, through quick defeats in France, breaking Versailles, remilitarising the Rhineland and Anschluss.
Army	Posed a major danger to the Nazi leadership if it felt threatened, so left structurally largely unchanged until 1938, despite an increase in size. 1937 – 'Hossbach Memorandum' received a cold reaction, where Hitler's expansionist vision was	Generally cooperating, having shared Hitler's anti-Bolshevism and anti-democracy; the increase of army twentyfold between 1933-9 and conscription was mutually beneficial. Foreign policy successes gave the army prestige previously lost.

outlined. General Beck stood in opposition to the increasing authoritarianism of the Nazi regime and Hitler's aggressive foreign policy. It was due to public foreign policy disagreements with Hitler that Beck resigned as Chief of Staff in August 1938	Hitler consolidated his control of the army after the death of Hindenburg and Night of the Long Knives in 1934, where the army pledge swore an oath of absolute obedience to him personally – the Blomberg-Fritz Affair in February 1938 also exploited problems in the army leadership and saw Hitler consolidate control.

Serious opposition may require:

- Organisation
- Strong leadership
- An alternative ideology
- Support from powerful groups

This was all very difficult during the period of the Nazi regime.

The Army had the strength and ability to effectively challenge the Nazi regime, but did not do so during the period of 1933-9 since Hitler's policies tended to be mutually beneficial; the Left had an alternative ideology yet the terror apparatus of the Nazi state restrained it from putting into place any meaningful action, and the example of the Night of the Long Knives in 1934 made it clear any leadership would be impossible; similarly, the Church struggled not only through the terror exerted by the Nazi state but also by the lack of consistency and solidarity within Churches against Nazism.

Broszat points to a different type of resistance. Rather than directly challenging the Nazi state, a non-serious type of opposition developed called *Resistenz*, effectively loyal reluctance. In his 1970s "Bavarian project" studying the micro-history of everyday life, he found nonconformity was widespread – such as women wearing valuable garments made of material that could be used for rearmament and trying different types of Weimar-style fashion versus the traditional values of being constrained to the domestic sphere. However, this was effectively not a powerful type of resistance – rather, it may indicate that the ideological control and indoctrination of the Nazis was not absolute and undermined the impact and authority of the Nazi regime.

Malmann and Paul disagree that this is resistance, but rather people wore fashionable clothes, lipstick, high heels or short dresses for themselves.

Resistance must be seen within the sphere of the Nazi propaganda and terror machines, together with the actual popularity of Nazi foreign and economic policies.

2. Efficiency of Nazi Regime 1933-39

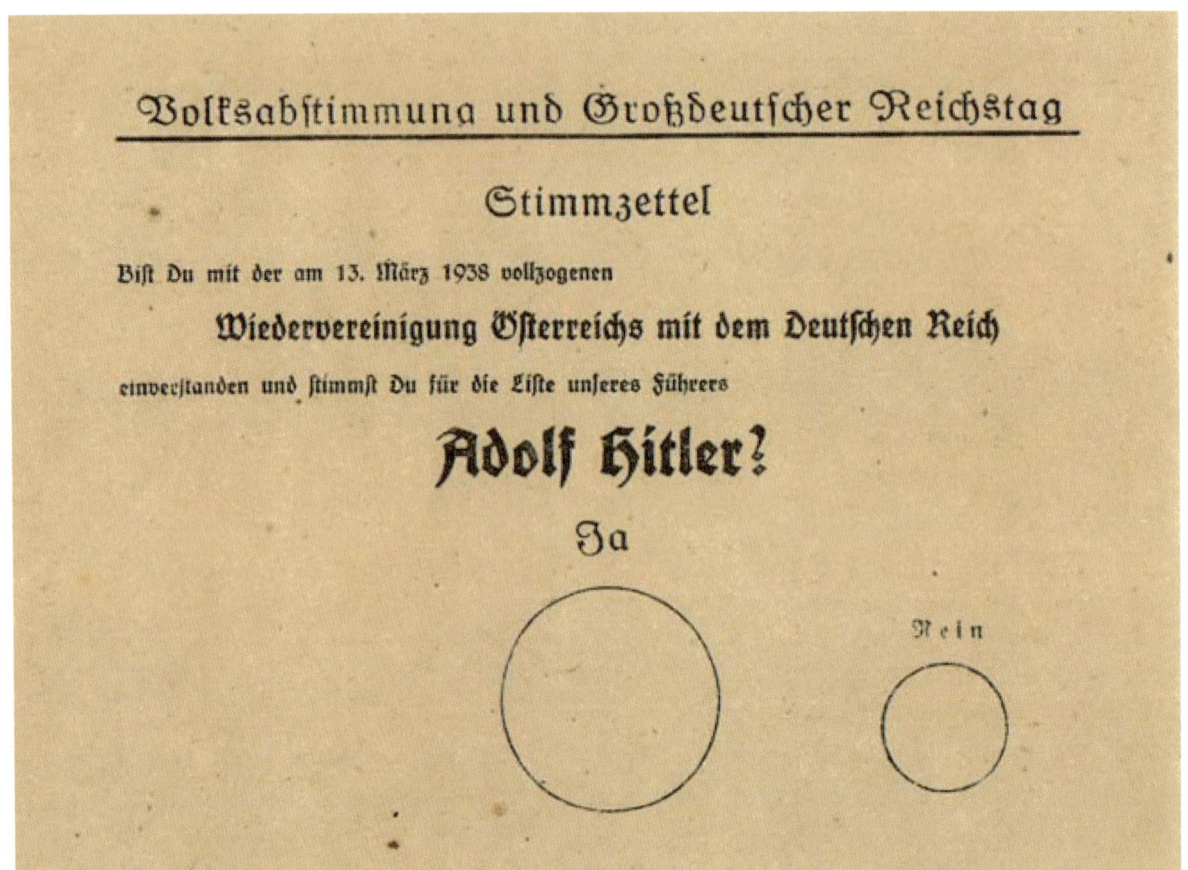

- *Polycratic, chaotic Nazi state*
- *"Working towards the Führer" in a feudal competition & cumulative radicalisation*
- *An opportunist dictator*
- *The effect of resistance*
- *Intentionalism v. structuralism historiography*

Was Hitler a master dictator?

	Yes	No
Political entrenchment; Gleichschaltung	Control over all major institutions	Polycracy and macro-management
	<ul><li>Night of the Long Knives</li><li>Hindenburg's death</li><li>Blomberg-Fritsch Affair</li><li>Unconditional obedience oath</li><li>Gleichschaltung; Nazification</li></ul>	<ul><li>Schacht v Goering</li><li>Vague directions, e.g. for rearmament - "German economy must be fit for war in four years"</li><li>Heydrich, Himmler and Goering: competition for police state</li></ul>
Realisation of ideological vision	Working towards the Führer	Opportunist dictator; constrainted
	<ul><li>Effectiveness of polycracy</li><li>Cumulative radicalisation; anti-Semitic policy</li><li>Aktion T4 euthanasia programme</li><li>When this did not work, e.g. Röhm SA, Strasser v SS confides – Hitler eradicated; Night of the Long Knives</li></ul>	<ul><li>Foreign policies opportunism; Mason – had to go to war</li><li>Anti-Semitic policies based on opportunism; Nuremberg Laws went against instincts</li><li>Constrained by popular pressures – working towards Führer sometimes failed, e.g. crucifix crisis</li></ul>
Use of propaganda	Effective propaganda machine	Ineffectual; required Goebbels
	<ul><li>Radio, film, press, rallies</li><li>Simple message reinforced several times</li><li>Evidence many Germans influenced, e.g. Gellately – "self surveillance state"</li></ul>	<ul><li>Art exhibitions and theatre ineffective modes of propaganda</li><li>Evidence not wholly effective:</li><li>Many workers in illegal left wing groups; Church opposition; conservatives' opposition.</li><li>Unhelped by confused and contradictory policy, e.g. women</li><li>Hitler could not act alone</li></ul>
Requirement of popular support	Almost unconditional support	Required support to act
	Achieved – plebiscites: March 1933 election success; Rhineland occupation referendum 98.8%, with 99% turnout; 1938 Reichstag elections w Austria 99% 'yes'	<ul><li>Weber – charismatic dictator; always required achievements to continue – esp. foreign policy</li><li>Hitler dependent on propaganda and terror, and even then not fully a master dictator</li></ul>

Was the Nazi state 1933-9 chaotic and incoherently governed?

How efficient was the Nazi Regime?

Termed by Tim Mason	Intentionalism	Structuralism
	Hitler had a clear world view and the aims of it were defined in Mein Kampf. He remained consistent to these aims throughout his political life There were moments when there was deviation from Hitler's programme but they were only for pragmatic reasons Hitler was all powerful and central to all events from 1933-1945 All political decisions were made by Hitler; the Nazi state was a monocratic state There was political infighting and chaos but this was a deliberate policy of divide and rule - Goldhagen: popular opinion in Germany was already sympathetic to a policy of Jewish extermination before the Nazi party came to power; Germany enthusiastically welcomed the persecution of Jews by the Nazi regime in the period 1933–39. - Brietman: Hitler had decided on the Holocaust early, as shown by his "prophesy" speech	The key to explaining domestic and foreign policy developments was the context within which Hitler and other decision makers operated There were agencies, power blocs and individuals that competed in a chaotic structure This chaos existed because Hitler was unwilling to create an ordered system of government and because there was a lack of clear planning and direction This chaotic competition explains the radicalisation of policy up until 1945 - Mason: Hitler had to go to war based on working class resentment - Broszat: the Holocaust began "bit by bit" as German officials stumbled into genocide - Browning: the "crooked path" to genocide; rivalry within the unstable Nazi power structure provided the major driving force behind the Holocaust but only after the failure of other schemes did they resort to genocide
	Synthesis of intentionalism and structuralism: Kershaw – "working towards the Führer" and cumulative radicalisation – Nazi policy was a result of pressures that came from both above and below and Hitler lacked a master plan, but was the decisive force behind policy.	

	Efficient based on Führer's will	Chaotic and competitive Nazi state
Hitler's bohemian lifestyle		Hitler uninvolved in governance
	Hitler was by instincts an artist and from 1935 he lived in a way that did not conform to normal patterns. He spent next to no time on administration of the government. When in Berlin he would take lunch and then meet with dignitaries for no more than an hour in the afternoon. He would then take a walk, eat supper and watch films (his favourites included Disney cartoons). Guests would often be subjected to a lengthy monologue on Hitler's favourite themes before he retired to bed, sometimes as late as 2am. Hitler did not like Berlin, preferring the mountain air and sensational views from his retreat in Bavaria. There his routine was none too strenuous. He would emerge just before noon to read extracts from the newspapers. A lengthy vegetarian lunch would be followed by an afternoon walk down the hill for tea and cakes. During the day he would occasionally deal with matters that were brought to his attention, but they would often be trivial. From 1934 Hitler showed little interest in decision making. The number of cabinet meetings declined from 72 in 1933 to none in 1938. Hitler rarely read important documents before making a decision and disliked signing official papers. Instead subordinates sought a verbal agreement or a nod of the Fuhrer's head.	
Economy	Working towards the Führer	Inefficient economic management
	Hitler had selected the leader he believed would best allow his will, and through "divide and rule" management this was possible. Production massively increased, in line with Hitler's aims to rearm, through the Hermann Goering Steelworks and rearmament programmes to achieve Autarky. Hitler knew that Goering was an ideological ally, while Schacht a less committed Nazi – having never had a meeting with him in his life. Thus, to actualise his will he best trusted Goering to do so; he would then produce policy that would undermine Schacht and better achieve this.	Hitler allowed Schacht free reign from 1933-1936 to reduce unemployment. However Hitler undermined him when he sanctioned the Four Year Plan led by Goring. Goring had stated his willingness to make Germany an Autarky and begin the rearmament process, whereas Schacht expressed hesitancy. Goring undermined Schacht so much that he resigned from his post in 1937. He was replaced by Funk who was willing to subordinate the Ministry of Economics to the Four Year Plan. By 1939, the economy was subject to many weaknesses.

	Hitler effectively commanded	Inefficient management
Foreign Policy	All foreign policy was effectively commanded by Hitler; the army having taken an oath of absolute obedience to the Führer and Hitler consolidating his control of the army after the Blomberg-Fritsch Affair and death of President Hindenburg.	Goering involved in Anschluss, phoning the Austrian Chancellor and suggesting to Hitler the idea of an ultimatum and plebiscite. Opposition by army, such as the resignation of Ludwig Beck in 1938.
	Hitler effectively commanded	Other Nazis controlled
The Terror State	Consolidates SS as primary police group after the Night of the Long Knives 1934 at his command; Hitler's decision to begin the Aktion T4 programme – doctors then begin to work towards the Führer, and cumulative radicalisation occurs. The SS-Gestapo complex aim to "work towards the Führer"; in this, it was effective in crushing opposition to the regime.	Feudal competition of Himmler and Heydrich; Philip Bouhler controlled the mailroom and worked towards the Führer in presenting letters of his choice – Hitler not a master dictator; Aktion T4 a secretive programme eventually ended based on popular criticism.
	Hitler effectively commanded	Acted within structures
Anti-Semitic policy	When he told young SA members to stop intuitive violence in August 1935, it did so. Indeed, the Nuremberg Laws of 1935 were announced by Hitler, and the 1933 Jewish Boycott was largely of his making. Through Hitler's close confidant Goebbels, violence such as that of Reichkristallnacht could be presented as intuitive and popular.	Hitler had to agree to the 1933 Boycott only being one day upon Schacht's concerns of the German economy; the Nuremberg Laws of 1935 were enacted against his best instincts as violence of the SA against Jews in public was unpopular.

3. Popularity of the Nazi Regime 1933-39

- A consensus dictatorship
- A product of propaganda and indoctrination
- A terroristic dictatorship
- Cult of the Führer: the Hitler Myth and state paternalism
- Success in creating a Volksgemeinschaft?
- Passive acceptance – few Germans were committed Nazis

(!) Difficult since it is unlikely Germans had a real outlet for opposition in a terror state

Did Hitler rely more on popular policy or propaganda?

Hence, was Hitler's dictatorship one of consensus or consent?

	Popular policy (consensus)	Propaganda (consent)
+	<ul><li>Popular foreign policies – re-establishing Germany post-Versailles</li><li>"Winning the battle for work"</li><li>Need for a "strong leader"</li><li>Respectability of Hitler after meeting Hindenburg</li><li>Goldberg – the popularity of anti-Semitic policy</li><li>Volksgemeinschaft policies</li><li>Hitler's Weberian charismatic leadership based on continual popular policy</li><li>"Working towards Führer" meant unpopular policy disassociated with Führer; e.g. 1937, crucifix crisis</li><li>Gellately – 'self surveillance society'</li></ul>	<ul><li>Procured the Hitler myth; widespread radio, enjoyable films (esp. Triumph of the Will 1935, winning even awards in Paris) and impressive rallies</li><li>Even grumbles about the regime were not directed towards Führer</li><li>DAF and KdF schemes popularity vindicated through propaganda, e.g Volkswagen</li><li>Nazis maintained a sense of terror through propaganda despite having the means to control the entire population (as Gellately shows statistically); Gramsci – terror must be combined with coercion</li></ul>
–	<ul><li>Unlikely anti-Semitic policy was genuinely popular</li><li>Quality of life significantly lowered through economic policy and rearmament</li><li>Opposition seen from churches, organiations of the left, youth groups</li><li>Evans 'pervasive terror state'</li><li>Cannot assume policies were popular – one could be arrested for not greeting with "Heil Hitler"</li></ul>	<ul><li>Some propaganda clearly ineffective – e.g. art galleries, concerts.</li><li>Failure of propaganda to truly infiltrate the population seen through a) the NEED for a terror state and thousands imprisoned b) the opposition seen despite a hugely coercive terror state</li></ul>

7. Life in Wartime Germany 1939-45

a) Military progress of World War 2
b) Opposition during the war
c) The wartime economy
d) Propaganda during the war
e) Development of the "Final Solution"

Bodies in Dresden

a) Military Progress of WW2

I. Invasion of France, 1940
II. Operation Barbarossa, 1941
III. Declaration of war on USA, 1941
IV. Stalingrad, 1942
V. D-Day, 1944
VI. Destruction of Germany, 1945

I. Invasion of France, 1940

The army leadership developed a strategy to invade through Belgian, but Hitler thought the plan too conventional – he instead developed a plan to drive panzer regiments through the wooded Ardennes, achieving an unexpected and surprise victory.

II. Operation Barbarossa, 1941

The Nazi decision broke the Nazi-Soviet pact of Aug 1939, as Hitler invaded the Soviet Union at his command. The army leadership supported the gamble, sharing Hitler's ethnic attitude to Slave and hatred of communism. They began drawing up invasion plans in July 1940, as part of working towards the Führer; nevertheless, the decision to invade was Hitler's alone, made conclusively in December 1940. He contradicted the army leadership on targeting Moscow, and instead decided to destroy the USSR's material base.

III. Declaration of war on USA, 1941

Again, a crucial example because it can be plausibly argued that Germany was unable to fight both the USSR and USA in reality. During 1941, Japan had been anxious before attacking the USA to negotiate a treaty with Germany – signed in December, all points were checked with the Führer by von Ribbentrop and the agreement merely committed Germany to not conclude a peace treaty with the USA without mutual consent between Germany and Japan.

Germany did not need to declare war on the US after Pearl Harbour, but it was Hitler's decision – regarding American involvement in the European war as inevitable and needing to retain the initiative, bolstering his Myth as a strong and decisive dictator.

IV. Stalingrad, 1942

Encirclement and destruction of Sixth Army at Stalingrad, and the loss of 250,000 men, can be traced back to Hitler's own decision. He over-committed his forces; the army was unallowed to withdraw – Hitler began to believe his own myth. After this failure, Hitler became openly criticised and the Hitler Myth began to erode.

V. D-Day, 1944

By 1944, German victories had given way to defeat in the East; Hitler had turned more and more to blaming the army leadership and this led to greater micro-management of the war – having already appointed himself in December 1941 Supreme Commander of the army. Army leaders in occupied France were unable to deploy panzer regiments positioned directly outside Paris without the Führer's direct permission; this delay proved highly significant.

VI. Destruction of Germany, 1945

As Hitler said in December 1944, "We'll never capitulate. Never. We can go down."; Hitler understood defeat was inevitable but aimed to avoid another humiliating surrender akin to that of 1918. Hitler's decree on 19th March 1945 for 'Destructive Measures on Reich Territory' was not implemented because Speer (having been Hitler's chief architect) persuaded a number of Gauleiters and military commanders to bypass it. By this point, Hitler's authority and the Hitler Myth was undermined. Hitler's power was gone as the war was lost; his Weberian charismatic leadership no longer upheld by foreign policy successes.

Failures of Germany and Total War

- One of the commonest explanations of Germany's defeat is that it failed to fight a fully 'total war' – an obvious example given is to say that Germany did not use its man and woman power as effectively as the British and Soviets did. Indeed, Goebbels was increasingly concerned by governmental inefficiency, from 1942 lobbying hard to be given powers to change this – Hitler did see the need for efficiency, but was more concerned with his personal political position.
- In 1943, the Committee of Tree aimed to scour Germany's bureaucracy for manpower – it contained Hitler's ultra loyalists. However, Goering, Goebbels and Speer met secretly – concerned about the committee and its potential rivalry to their power bases – to undermine it and Hitler's confidence, apparently without consideration for the war effort. The 'committee' consequently met eleven times and achieved nothing of significance.
- In July 1944, Goebbels' repeated lobbying found success, and he was appointed Reich Plenipotentiary for the Total War Effort – Goebbels could boast 'full dictatorial powers'. However, the military was excluded from decrees and he could only issue decrees to others of the highest Reich authorities who then could only issue subsequent decrees. Total war became a bureaucratic mess, adding to the incoherent competition of the feudal system. Nevertheless, it was Hitler who retained full dictatorial powers.

b) Opposition during the war

i. To what extent was there significant morale during the war?
ii. Why did the German people 'fight to the end'?
iii. To what extent was opposition widespread or significant?

Change over time: military turning points and morale

Invasion of France, 1940

Prior to the invasion, there had been widespread anxiety. However, as the campaign progressed, the SS reported 'admiration for the achievements of the German troops is boundless'. After the defeat of the French, the announcement was greeted by spontaneous demonstrations and an atmosphere of general jubilation (Evans), as what had been intended during WWI had been achieved so quickly – war veterans had been astonished as long-held nationalist dreams were vindicated. This marked the highest point of Hitler's popularity during the Third Reich.

Operation Barbarossa, 1941

Most Germans were surprised, since unlikely previous attacks it was not preceded by hostile propaganda (since the attack was a surprise to the Russians too); many worried Hitler was biting off more than he could chew. Nevertheless, the alliance with Bolshevism was undesirable to many and the news of war was in some sense relieving. Hitler did ultimately lose popularity with the prospect of a longer war as WWI.

Defeat at Stalingrad, 1943

As defeat approached, "even faith in Hitler began to fade" amongst the soldiers in Stalingrad. The SS reported a feeling of deep shock, with many seeing it as the 'beginning of the end', and scornful of rhetoric in official propaganda.

Everyday life responses to war

- Food rationing

In October 1939, an official food ration of 2570 calories a day was set for civilians. This fell during the war. Bread fell from 10 kilos to 3.6kilos per month in April 1945; meat fell from 2400 grams to 550 grams by April 1945. There were similar reductions in cereals and fats. These were insufficient for most people's needs, reducing consumption to a quarter of peacetime levels by late 1941. The use of synthetic (ersatz) was particularly undesirable.

- Sex as a commodity

By 1944, sex was becoming a commodity with young women in particular bartering it or foodstuffs and luxuries such as chocolate or cigarettes; this was in direct contradiction with traditional values and propagandist message, especially when the sex was with 'racial inferiors'.

- Reactions to Goebbels' Total War speech in 1943

Had little of a mobilisation impact, failing to convince people since the desperation of ordinary life meant people already knew economic mobilisation had gone about as far as it could.

- Reactions to Allied bombing

a) Breakdown of ordinary life – a sanitary officer in Hamm January 1945 stated 'they are grabbing at other people's possessions, they don't respect women and children' – social disorder was rampant.

b) Criticisms of the leadership – popular jokes criticised the leadership, and in 1943 someone in Dusseldorf hung a picture of Hitler from a home-made gallows, albeit this was a strongly working class left-wing area. According to Evans, discontent had easily come to the surface in these towns since belief in the Nazi system had never deeply penetrated the masses. Hitler had famously promised before that no bomb would fall on Germany, undermining the Hitler Myth.

c) Comparative lack of hostility towards the Allies – only 1% of captured Allied airmen were lynched or shot. The SS commented that hate-filled words against England were often an expression of desperation, but one could not speak of hatred for the English people as a whole.

Why was widespread opposition not effectively channelled or effective?

In Italy, Mussolini was removed as Prime Minister by the President in July 1943 after Rome was bombed and it was clear the Axis was at a loss. This did not happen in Germany for a number of reasons:

- Hitler was both Chancellor and President; he was the Führer
- Goebbels and "Total War"
- Difficulty in access to Hitler; protected by SS and mine fields in the Wolf's Lair
- Propaganda portrayal as a "war of annihilation" against racial subhumans
- Fear of revenge from Russia and Poland, given the torture and genocide war crimes unleashed on both countries
- Feudal polycratic competition – no governmental cohesion; leadership cannot work together to rid of Hitler
- The army swore an unconditional oath of obedience to the Führer, and could use this to justify failing to stop fighting
- Fear of Nazi terror – the Gestapo-SS complex was extremely reactive should any public resistance be shown. Hitler Youth also contributed, for example killing 100 people for surrendering on the last day of war.

Group	Effective opposition	Ineffective opposition
Church	Continued to be interested in self-defence, albeit Catholics had moral concerns over racial policy. von Galen's Aktion T4 speech 1941 – effectively ended public euthanasia programme	Men were conscripted – only women could resist, and they even themselves believed to be confined to the domestic sphere. Failure to effectively condemn the extermination of the Jews
Left	Opposition came from individuals and underground groups; Red Orchestra formed to spy on Nazis for the USSR; resistance cells were formed in factories; by 1941 in Berlin alone there were 89 of these cells; pamphlets attacked the regime.	Undermined by Nazi-Soviet Pact August 1939 - June 1941; the Nazis in WWII were effectively fighting *with* socialism rather than against it. However, after Operation Barbarossa this changed. Large organisations or activities would easily be penetrable by the Gestapo, hence the left had to rely on only the activities of small illegal groups and individuals. The Red Orchestra was particularly vulnerable to infiltration, and was devastated in 1943.
Youth	Aimed to oppose the group militarism of Hitler Youth, especially after the 1942 failures of WWII; absence or loss of fathers increased juvenile delinquency. Many repelled by the brutality of the regime actively rebelled; the Edelweiss Pirates attacked Hitler Youth members and Munich Students formed the White Rose group.	These groups were also vulnerable to Gestapo infiltration; in 1943 leaders of the White Rose group Scholls led an anti-Nazi Munich demonstration; in February, they were arrested and publicly executed by the Gestapo.
Conservatives	Primarily drawn from conscience, but after military success dwindled from 1942 this opposition became more significant. Many demanded the restoration of rights and freedoms. The Kreisau Circle from 1941 drew together those critical of the regime, containing an ideological spread of autocrats	The group had few activities, since its meetings and existence was in secret; moreover they were split over most things. It included two Jesuit priests, two Lutheran pastors, conservatives, liberals, monarchists, landowners, former trade-union leaders and diplomats. Moltke favoured a federal EU, where Goerdeler wanted Germany as an independent state within Europe; few could agree between state

	and socialists; there was no cohesive replacement ideology. Members worked to inform western Allies such as the United Kingdom about political changes in the regime.	ownership and private property. Nevertheless, they were united in their desire for a humane Germany. In 1944, they were discovered by the Gestapo; no coup plan had been formulated, but some of the remaining members were involved in the Bomb Plot that year.
Army	The Nazis ultimately aimed to win WWII and prevent a repeat of WWI. Many of the Prussian military elite were too upper class to support Nazism. This led von Stauffenberg, a military elite, during 1944 when it became clear Germany was losing the war to help devise a bomb plot. Having seen the treatment of the Jews and Slavs in Russia, together with German troops, he labelled Hitler the antichrist and was willing to kill Hitler. He had to kill Himmler and Hitler at the same time, else Himmler would just take his place; the first attempt was aborted when Himmler was not present, since Nazis purposely moved around often. The aim was to kill Hitler and then establish a coup d'état that would see Ludwig Beck take over as Head of State, having resigned in opposition to Hitler in 1938. The coup would have to see Friedrich Fromm, Head of the Reserve Army – who had not indicated support or lack thereof in the plot – give the Valkyrie order to mobilise troops on the street. Hundreds of officers were involved in the conspiracy a year after Stalingrad.	Only acted when it was clear Germany was losing the war; failed to give any real opposition during the period of 1939-43. Indeed, the loyalty shown by key Nazis to Hitler meant that the Bomb Plot failed to reach any actual Nazis; the coup could not gain any public support since it was secret. In failing to kill Hitler by chance, Fromm refused to give the order and instead the men were killed. The failure to act was justified through the "oath of loyalty", with swathes of Nazis having committed war crimes and genocide clearly concerned about the repercussions of their actions in a non-Nazi state.

c) The wartime economy

The outbreak of war in September 1939 saw the responsibility for the planning of the German war economy shared among competing agencies in the 'feudal competition':

- The Ministry of War, General Thomas led the economics section in charge of the armaments programme
- The Ministry of Economics, led by Walter Funk
- The Four Year Plan, plenipotentiary Hermann Goering
- In March 1940, a Ministry of Munitions was created under Fritz Todt ending some of the confusion in control of production

	Successes and achievements of economy	Weaknesses and failures of economy
1939-42	Operation Barbarossa saw military expenditure rise from 17.2m RM to 56m RM in 1942. The numbers working in aircraft manufacturing doubled between 1939-41 Use of French prisoners of war partly made up the shortfall of labour, with some 800,000 by October 1940, and other nationals (mainly Poles) making a total of 2m foreign workers in Germany by the end of the year. By the end of 1942, this rose to 6.4m foreign workers as the Vichy government in France established compulsory labour for men and women aged 18-65.	Economy not fully mobilised for war in this period – Blitzkrieg wars did not place great demands on economic production. Output per head 1939-40 fell 13% mainly because of the effects of conscription and concentration on consumer industries Even as military expenditure increased, a shortage of labour became evident. By May 1940 there were 3.5m fewer workers than the year before – affected deeply by conscription. 1.7m conscripted 1941, and a further 1.4m before May 1942.
1942-45	In February 1942, Speer was appointed Todt's successor as Minister for Weapons and Munitions; he developed plans for the rationalisation of industry and more efficient control of raw material distribution. Total War was initiated by a speech by Goebbels in February 193,	Economic performance remained incoherently organised. There were too many competing agencies for consistent policy to be formulated. When clear logic was developed from the center, it countered economic logic; until Nazi militarism was eventually defeated, its aims were largely supported by the industrial and financial world:

calling for universal labour service and closing of 8,000 non-essential businesses

Speer established the Armaments Commission in 1943 to attempt to standardise production, allowing mass production – better floor space led to the production of the Me109 plane in Messerschmitt increasing from 180p/m to 1,000p/m in just three factories. The types of vehicle production was reduced from 55 to 14, resulting in greater productivity.

Central control of raw materials also helped see a rise in output per head 32% higher in 1943 than in 1939. Production times were introduced, for example the Panzer III tank reduced in assembly time by 50%.

Despite an increase in workforce of only 11% between 1939-44, production of all weapons grew by 130%.

Increases in expenditure and production techniques brought significant increases in productivity during this period.

- Looting of conquered countries undertaken systematically by companies such as chemicals giant IG Farben, becoming the largest chemical producer in Europe by 1942 and seeing their profits doubled from 1936.

From January 1945, the German economy was in a state of collapse – partly due to invasion but also due to exhaustion and the effects of Allied bombing hitting industrial centres and taking away workers. In 1944, German military expenditure reached 115% of net domestic product.

Social policies also undermined economic policies – foreign powers had productivity rates 60-80% lower than that of German workers; from 1940, Polish workers had to wear 'P' armbands and were forbidden from using public transport. However in March 1944 all Eastern workers were given the same pa and benefits as other foreign labours in a last-ditch attempt to increase productivity; poor treatment had already ultimately failed to solve Germany's foreign labour problems.

Lack of law materials – Germany had a massive lack of natural resources, above all reserves of high-quality iron ore. Goering attempted to develop production of low grade ore for manufacturing purposes, yet this could never meet the demands of expanding military needs – making Germany largely dependent on imports. This levelled at about 5.5m tones annually from neutral Sweden. However, annexed lands did eventually lead to increased access to natural resources; this policy ultimately failed due to the failure of military Blitzkreig from 1942. Germany failed to fully utilise the natural resources of annexed lands.

Lack of female labour – between 1939-44 only 200,000 extra women entered the workforce. Hitler ideologically refused to

		allow conscription of women – even after Total War was proclaimed; only another 400,000 women were recruited for work. Speer had attempted to correct this, but Hitler refused full-scale mobilisation. Women had been encouraged to child bear, and hence had responsibilities for their new large families. 89% of single women were in employment, contrasted with 52% of all women; there were already a significant number of women in the workforce from the Weimar period, too.

"Kinder, Küche, Kirche"

- German economy did not expand sufficiently to meet the demands of 'total war'
- This was due to many factors:
    o Chaotic polycracy; the failure of a consistent economic policy
    o Lack of natural resources
    o Failure to utilise female labour
    o Ideological and social policies
        ▪ Murder of 6m Jews while trying to find labour;
        ▪ Mistreated foreign workers

d) Goebbels and Propaganda during the war

The role of Josef Goebbels 1939-45

After the defeat of Stalingrad in 1943, Goebbels played a major role in organising Germany's domestic war effort – he toured bombed cities, raising morale and organising relief. His February 1943 speech proclaiming 'total war' is infamous. He was made General Plenipotentiary for the Mobilisation of Total War to organise all manpower intended to stave off the Soviet advance. At the end of the war, he persuaded Hitler to make his dramatic suicide, poisoning his children and shooting his wife.

- Film

On the evening of 30 January 1945, a prestigious film premiere came on the twelfth anniversary of Hitler's seizure of power – Goebbels' latest propaganda spectacular. It told the story of the defence of a small German town during the Napoleonic Wars. It was produced in impressive Afgacolour, with battle scenes of hitherto unrivalled grandeur. It was the most expensive film of the Third Reich – costing 80.5m RM. Six thousand horses were employed, and a hundred railway wagons full of salt – the aim was to create the 'biggest movie of all time'. The enormous expense was justified during the most critical stage of war through Goebbels' belief that its message of honourable sacrifice and popular solidarity of resistance would galvanise German citizens in the war.

However a deep irony existed in that the impending crisis of the war meant only a tiny minority of Germans had the time, the opportunity or the inclination to see the film; the young and old were being conscripted, and few cinemas were left from air raids – others closed due to a lack of coal for hearing. Indeed, three days after its release the very scene of its premiere, Alexanderplatz, was a smouldering mass of ruins.

In 1940, three anti-Semitic films were released to stress the Jewish problem, including *Der Ewige Jude* (the Eternal Jew) – presenting Jews as a parasitic race on the German nation. Few Germans enjoyed the film, and many found it horrific. The more subtle films were more effective.

- Speeches

In January, it became clear to the German public that Stalingrad had been a disaster with many German casualties. Goebbels had the difficult job of facing the German public on the ten year anniversary of the Nazi seizure of power, 30 January 1943. He rose to the occasion, delivering an impassioned and rousing speech to cheers and

enthusiasm from the crowd; even as air-raid sirens sounded toward the end of the speech, Goebbels recalled that 'Nobody got up from his place'.

After Goebbels' Total War speech, he had urged other propaganda departments across Germany to report on the reaction to the speech. The preliminary response was praise for his handling of the 'Jewish question'; from Bochum in the Ruhr it was reported that one district leadership of the party called for the deportation of Jews. Not disappointed, on the 27 February an operation to deport German Jews began – within a few days 7,000 deported from the capital, in an acceleration of their persecution.

Total War saw the conscription of young (including Hitler Youth) and old, together with the use of labour of women. Goebbels proclaimed he would unleash Germany's hitherto hidden military power. A slogan developed of "Enjoy the war; peace will be dreadful"; air raids continued, with Americans shelling cities during the day and the British at night. People were brought together to work under the bombs, but nevertheless morale declined as destitution worsened. Goebbels had increasing public visibility as Hitler began to take a back-seat role.

- Other media

Photographs of Katyn Forest murders

In Spring 1943, Goebbels received a propaganda opportunity for the war – the news in early April that German forces had uncovered the bodies of thousands of Polish officers in mass graves in the Katyn Forest; it was quickly established the Poles had been murdered by Soviet police. Since the Stalingrad defeat, Goebbels had aimed to present the prospect of a Europe dominated by 'Bolshevik hordes' where dissidents would be liquidated. He secured Hitler's consent for the fullest exploitation of the massacre, arranging for Polish and foreign journalists to attend and take photographs – these were published all over Europe, in the hope that this would create a genuine division in Allied forces and strengthen anti-Bolshevik feeling.

e) Development of the "Final Solution"

In assessing the development of the "final solution", one may contrast and compare the relative influence of the four below factors.
- The Führer's will and vision
- The chaotic, polycratic feudal competition
- Attitudes of ordinary Germans
- The effect of war

Chronology of the "final solution"

Pre-war policy	1933 Jewish Boycott; 1935 Nuremberg Laws; 1938 Reichkristallnacht
30 Jan 1939 *The Prophesy*	Hitler spoke to a packed and expectant Reichstag, revealing the link he had made between war and racial struggle; he alluded to the power of an International Jewry, and a military struggle to win the Aryan people living space. He warned that, should Jews succeed in plunging Europe into another world war, they would see the annihilation of their race in Europe. However this was not a clear-cut plan for the 'Jewish problem', nor was any coherent policy in existence; there was not, either, the necessary environment for the annihilation of Jews that Hitler spoke of.
Start of WW2	Led to further restrictions on Jews. On 1 September 1939, a curfew was introduced for all Jews, and on 21 September Heydrich ordered the concentration of Jews around railway junctions. Radio sets were confiscated from Jews, as they were increasingly excluded from mainstream society. On 1 September 1941 all Jews were ordered to wear a Start of David badge; in April 1943, all German Jews lost their German citizenship.
Sep 1939	On the advent of war, and the intended destruction of a supposed International Jewry, Poland was successfully taken under Nazi rule, as was much of western Europe in 1940. Consequently, millions more Jews were brought under direct Nazi rule. In January 1940 the Jews were used for slave labour and confined to ghettos in the previously Polish towns of Warsaw, Lodz and Lublin.
Summer 1940	The final solution to the Jewish question in the minds of most leading Nazis was a territorial one. By the summer of 1940, Heydrich was suggesting that 3¼ Jews under German control should be moved elsewhere; the Foreign Office suggested Madagascar. Hitler was openly enthusiastic about the scheme, discussing it with Mussolini in June 1940. Clearly Madagascar could not sustain the Jewish population of Europe, thus the policy of effective annihilation was ell being considered. However, it required defeating the British for control of the high seas

June 1941	The early success of the invasion of the Soviet Union further increased the number of Jews under Nazi control, raising the policy of relocating Europe's Jews to the East. Nazi propaganda stressed the war against the USSR was one of annihilation against racial subhumans; it was to achieve the destruction of communism and the gaining of Lebensraum for the Aryan people. The destruction of Russian Jews came as a consequence of this policy, with Eastern Jews seen as the lowest race of all. In June, as Nazi troops swept across the western Soviet Union, SS Einsatzgruppen were authorised by Hitler to exterminate Jews – giving the order to treat Jews as partisans; eight months later 700,000 had been brutally murdered.
Autumn 1941	The Nazi regime remained undecided about the final solution. Shooting Jews had been the preferred option, but was not a realistic option in German-dominated Europe both due to the psychological trauma complained of by the SS and the scope of Jews making it too bloody an operation. Deporting Jews remained difficult, and required success in defeating the USSR. Hitler deliberated the fate of the Jews up until September 1941, but this changed for several reasons. Firstly, in August 1941 Stalin ordered the deportation to Siberia of 600,000 ethnic Germans in the Volga region. Roosevelt's order of September said the US Navy was to shoot German warships on sight.
September to November 1941	*Deportations* The German advance slowed on the Eastern front as summer turned to autumn; Hitler realised he could not wait until 1942 to deal with the Jewish question, with conditions in the East pressuring action – all Gauleiter in Poland anxious to remove Jews from their territories – moving them between each other and creating tension. By late 1941, pressure came from Gauleiter in the west (including Goebbels) that they be allowed to deport their Jews, triggering demands from those in the East. On 16 September, Hitler and Himmler discussed the deportations, and the order was given for the deportations to the East, promising further deportations eastwards. Kershaw has argued the decision to deport Jews eastwards brought the Holocaust a massive step further. *Initiatives in the East* Hitler's agreement to deport Jews saw regional Nazi leaders to seize initiative in Poland. In October, the police chief of Lublin ordered the construction of gassing facilities at Belzec. In Lodz Jews were being short and gassed. Additionally, Hans Frank – Gauleiter of the Central Government – was concerned his region was being used by Heydrich as a dumping ground for Jews.

	This was partly due to directives from the Nazi leadership. In October, the Gestapo Chief Müller published Himmler's order that no Jew be allowed to leave the Reich. On 21 November, the Führer demanded an 'aggressive policy' to rid Berlin of Jews; Goebbels' propaganda inspired hatred.
	Confusion persisted in the 'Jewish question' as 5,000 German Jews were shot on Lithuania while in Lodz the Germans worried about sanitary conditions in the overcrowded ghettos.
December 1941	The final turning point was the declaration of war against the USA on 11 December 1941. On 12 December, Hitler evoked his 'prophecy', with this the stage of war it was now applicable – on 18 December Hitler told Himmler that the Jews were to be 'exterminated as partisans'; since Russian Jews were already being shot, this could only mean the annihilation of all German Jews. Indeed, from January 1942 onwards there was a ruthless enforcement of final solution policy indicative of a clear decision having been made.
January 1942 Wannsee Conference	This conference was chaired by Heydrich, and a key stepping-stone on the road to the final solution. Heydrich attempted to coordinate the various bodies of Nazi government into agreement about the steps taken next. It is clear a systematic programme for the annihilation of Europe's Jews had been formed by this point, and this conference was largely to consolidate Heydrich's leadership in the programme.
	At the conference, State Secretary of the Government General, Josef Bühler, asked that his area should have its Jews removed as quickly as possible. In the next few months, German Jews were deported to the ghettos in the east and then to the death camps of Treblinka, Sobibor and Auschwitz.
1942-5 Extermination	The network of concentration camps spread throughout these years. There were those within the SS such as Oswald Pohl who aimed to exploit the labour resource at hand; in charge of the development of the WVHA, the economic administration section of the SS, he had control of 20 concentration and 165 labour camps by 1942. A compromise developed in concentration camps wherein Jews would be used as labour but they would be worked to death.
	German industry systematically exploited this labour. IG Farben used Jewish labour at the huge Monowitz-Buna complex near Auschwitz. The systematic and industrial scale of murder was vast. At Auschwitz, over a million were murdered; Treblinka saw 800,000 murdered; to a total of six million. Even as late as July 1944 when resources for the war were hard pressed, Adolf Eichmann (head of the SS department concerned with Jewish affairs) had priority to use railways to transport Jews to their death. Ideology was put above practicalities, as was a major flaw in Germany's wartime economy.

The Führer's will and vision

- Hitler's ideological vision of Mein Kampf; racially pure Aryan Germany must fight the parasitic disease of inextricably linked Jewish Bolshevism
- Führerprinzp and the Hitler Myth: working towards the Führer
- 1939 prophesy
- Hitler's approval of the deportation to Madagascar policy in Summer 1940
- Einsatzgruppen authorised by Hitler to exterminate Eastern Jews in June 1941
- Personally deliberated the fate of the Jews until September 1941, until he authorised deportations after a meeting with Himmler that month
- Hitler evoked his 'prophesy' in December 1941 to see Jews 'exterminated as partisans', with a clear implication

The chaotic, polycratic feudal competition

- Chaotic, 'piecemeal' and slow murder had taken place in the East, while Lithuania Jews were being killed by local people appointed by Einsatzgruppe despite no formal policy being clear on the eradication of the Jews – this created an environment of cumulative radicalisation and dehumanisation of Jews
- Moreover, German leaders not only intended to "work towards the Führer" by providing anti-Semitic policy but Gauleiter wanted to protect their own area.
- From 1940, German Gauleiter in Poland had to deal with more Jews than their western counterparts – this frustrated individuals such as Hans Frank who believed his Central Government district was being used as a dumping ground for Jews by Heydrich after the directive from Himmler and Hitler in September to deport Jews eastwards. Heydrich in the Wannsee Conference pleases the Interior Ministry, Transport organisations, Four Year Plan representatives et cetera to effectively win the feudal competition on managing the final solution
- Prior to 1942 (Heydrich died that year), Heydrich had headed the SS-Gestapo complex; after this, it was Himmler. Heydrich had formed the Einsatzgruppen on Himmler's instructions, a death squad group intended to round up political opponents including Jews during the war.
- Speer refused to accept Himmler's offer of the high rank of SS-Oberst-Gruppenführer that Heydrich had, as he felt to do so would put him in Himmler's debt and obligate him to allow Himmler a say in armaments production. Himmler assumed Speer a dangerous rival, and indeed the radicalisation of anti-Semitic policy may in part be due to please Hitler in this regard – he was particularly loyal to the Führer, Hitler referring to him as "my loyal Himmler"
- This consequently led to initiatives being taken by eastern leaders attempting to eradicate their own 'Jewish questions' by using gassing and extermination policies.
- All attempted to please their own interests, leading to extreme policies such as Heydrich's of deporting the 11m Jews in all European countries developing.
- Nevertheless, this was ultimately derived from the Fuhrer's will

Attitudes of ordinary Germans

- Nazi propaganda presented a social-Darwinist message of Aryan racial superiority, and the self-containing Jews made an effective scapegoat for any German failures.
- They were blamed for the failure of WWI, and treated as a parasitic disease of Bolshevism through the propaganda of Goebbels – dehumanisation of Jews
- Many Germans were simply apathetic to the anti-Semitic policy; the church believed Jews had killed Christ, and their acceptance of homosexuality and liberalism emblematic of the fated modernity of the Weimar era

- The Nazi regime also never publicly identified itself with the exacting horror of the Holocaust
- Nevertheless there were reasons other than belief preventing real resistance
    - The all-pervasive terror state, incorporating the "state within a state" SS-Gestapo complex infiltrating and undermining all resistance
    - Limited actual knowledge of the level of industrial murder; merely an awareness of labour camps
    - German people were not targeted as ethnic Aryans; it was not seen as their problem
    - Those in the civil service were tasked with individual jobs rather than full-scale murder on their own accord; for example, to ensure the load of vans transporting Jews was not too heavy as to break the machinery – civil servants were ensured to have a detached style about them
    - Equally, the army's oath of obedience and Führerprinzp oaths of obedience including that of the Hitler Youth were used as justifications in fear of the repercussions of actions should military losses lead to Soviet and Allied victory

However, von Galen in 1941 spoke out against the euthanasia programme but similar Catholic rhetoric did not occur against the policy of the final solution. It is clear that at least to an extent Germans were uninterested and anti-Semitic in their nature.

The Goldhagen thesis suggests Germans carried out the mass extermination of Jews not because of the terror, traditions of obedience, peer pressure or career ambition but because they enjoyed killing Jews – they had a murderous and consuming hatred of Jews. However, Goldhagen has been criticised for a simplistic analysis that downplays opposition and the psychological trauma of executioners (leading to the development of gas chambers), differentiations between German classes and social groups and the massive terror instrument of the Nazi state.

Nevertheless, as Browning argues, Goldhagen's work is useful for having "retained a human element to the study of the Holocaust" – one cannot take the approach of merely studying Nazi leaders only.

The effect of war

- Acted more as a catalytic agent on final solution rather than a cause
- Poland was successfully taken under Nazi rule, as was much of western Europe in 1940. Consequently, millions more Jews were brought under direct Nazi rule
- In June 1941, as Nazi troops swept across the western Soviet Union, SS Einsatzgruppen were authorised by Hitler to exterminate Jews – giving the order to treat Jews as partisans; eight months later 700,000 had been brutally murdered.
- Hitler deliberated the fate of the Jews up until September 1941, but this changed for several reasons. Firstly, in August 1941 Stalin ordered the deportation to Siberia of 600,000 ethnic Germans in the Volga region. Roosevelt's order of September said the US Navy was to shoot German warships on sight
- As it became clear Germany was losing the war from 1942, the scale of murder seems to have drastically increased as Hitler intended to retain his control and the final solution had to be executed before the chance was lost

Exam information

1. Past paper exam questions

a) Essay questions on Germany 1900-33 and 1939-45

Second Reich 1900-14

- 'Power in the Second Reich lay in the hands of the traditional elites'. How far do you agree with this judgement?

- 'The threat of constitutional reform was the biggest problem facing the Second Reich'. How far do you agree with this judgement?

- 'Moderate reform caused the balance of power to remain unchanged'. How far do you agree with this judgement?

- 'WWI heightened rather than narrowed the problems that the Second Reich faced'. How far do you agree with this judgement?

- To what extent was Germany a parliamentary democracy from 1900-18?

Weimar Republic 1919-33

- 'The main threat to the existence of the Weimar Republic in the years 1919-1923 was its fated constitution' How far do you agree with this judgement?

- 'A period of instability followed by a period of stability' How far do you agree with this judgement of the Weimar Republic?

- 'Germany experienced a period of stability during the Stresemann years'. How far do you agree with this judgement?

- 'The Weimar Republic survived for so long because of economic policy successes'. How far do you agree with this judgement?

- 'Economic depression in 1929 highlighted the inherent weaknesses of the Weimar Republic' How far do you agree with this judgement?

The Rise of Hitler 1923-33

- 'The appeal to a Volksgemeinschaft explains the rapid growth in Nazi support by 1932' How far do you agree with this judgement?

- 'The economic depression of 1929 explains the rapid growth in Nazi support by 1932' How far do you agree with this judgement?

- 'Political intrigue [backhand schemes, e.g. of political elites von Papen and Hindenburg] explains why Hitler was able to become Chancellor in 1933' How far do you agree with this judgement?

- 'The Nazi consolidation of power in 1933 was caused by brutality and terror' How far do you agree with this judgement?

- 'The Nazi rise and consolidation of power by the end of 1933 was caused by the failure of communism to stop them'. How far do you agree with this judgement?

- 'The effects of the Wall Street Crash caused the Weimar Republic to give way to Hitler's regime'. How far do you agree with this judgement?

- 'Hitler had fully consolidated his power by the end of 1933'. How far do you agree with this judgement?

- 'Economic depression accounts for the failure of the Weimar Republic by the end of 1933' How far do you agree with this judgement?

- 'The failure of the Weimar Republic by 1933 was inevitable' How far do you agree with this judgement?

Germany at War 1939-45

- 'The main opposition during WWII came from the youth'. How far do you agree with this judgement?

- 'The war economy lacked the efficiency to meet the demands of total war'. How far do you agree with this judgement?

- 'Systematic extermination emerged as the Final Solution to the Jewish Question as a result of the chaotic nature of the Nazi state'. How far do you agree with this judgement?

- 'WWII highlighted the inherent weaknesses of the Nazi regime'. How far do you agree with this judgement?

b) Controversy questions on the Nazi Regime

- 'The Nazi regime depended more on its broad popularity than on terror in the years 1933–39.' How far do you agree with this opinion?
- 'The Nazi regime was popular because of Hitler's charismatic leadership.' How far do you agree with this opinion?
- 'The Nazi policy towards the Jews was plain and unwavering.' How far do you agree with this opinion?
- 'Hitler was a weak dictator.' How far do you agree with this opinion?
- 'In the years 1933-1939 Hitler's rule became a despotic tyranny'. How far do you agree with this opinion?
- 'The power of the Fuhrer was comprehensive and total'. How far do you agree with this opinion?
- How far do you agree that Hitler's Regime was a 'consensus dictatorship'?
- 'The Nazi regime enjoyed broad consent brought about by popular policies'

Explain your answer, using the evidence of the sources and your own knowledge of the issues related to this controversy.

Please look elsewhere for sources (Edexcel provided textbook, past papers) as they cannot be reproduced in this revision guide.

2. Exam technique

Section (A) – 30 marks, *50 minutes*

How to use the time

1. First 2 minutes of the exam
   - Plan the essay briefly,
   - Note links between different factors

2. Next 48 minutes of the exam
   - Spend 4 minutes writing an introduction
   - Spend 40 minutes on the main content (c. 10m per paragraph)
   - Spend 4 minutes writing a conclusion

Structure for the exam

Introduction

- Interpret the question, and define any key terms
- Point to line of argument, with brief reasons why
- Outline factors of consideration

Main body

Select 3-5 factors for a given question, beginning with the named factor if applicable and explain why one is the most important.

- Make a point that answers the question
- Give evidence and discussion in favour of this factor being important
- Give evidence and discussion against this factor being important
- Explain how the evidence as a whole supports the judgment of the point
- Link it back to the question and the line of argument in a sentence

Conclusion

- Explain line of argument
- Explain how this conclusion was reached, addressing any opposing ideas

Section (B) – 40 marks, *70 minutes*

How to use the time

1. First 5 minutes of the exam –
    - Read all of the sources
    - Briefly summarise after reading each source its argument
    - Write down the structure intended for the essay

2. Next 5 minutes of the exam –
    - Highlight which parts of each source agree with the question
    - Highlight which parts of each source disagree with the question
    - Briefly note additional knowledge to corroborate any of the points
    - If Section (A) overran, do this <u>during</u> the exam

3. Next 60 minutes of the exam –
    - Spend 5 minutes writing the introduction
    - Spend 16 minutes writing the first paragraph
    - Spend 16 minutes writing the second paragraph
    - Spend 16 minutes writing the third paragraph
    - Spend 7 minutes writing the conclusion

Structure for the exam

Introduction

- Interpret the question, and define any key terms and controversy question relates to
- Briefly outline the judgment of the three sources, and whether they agree or disagree with the question – offer an allusion to the final judgment of the essay

Paragraph 1 – agreeing with the question

- Construct an argument for the opinion in the question
- Explain which source largely agrees and how this source largely agrees with the opinion in the question
- Explain which sources agree with each other and how these sources agree with each other about the opinion in the question
- Use short quotes
- Use your own knowledge to provide further evidence to support the judgements of this argument
- Use your own knowledge to evaluate this argument

Paragraph 2 – disagreeing with the question

- Construct an argument against the opinion in the question
- Explain which source largely disagrees and how this source disagrees with the opinion in the question
- Explain which sources agree with each other and how these sources agree with each other in disagreeing with the opinion in the question
- Use small quotes
- Use your own knowledge to provide further evidence to support the judgements of this argument
- Use your own knowledge to evaluate this argument

Paragraph 3 – compromise with the question

- Construct an argument that covers a middle way (a combination of fpr and against the opinion in the question)
- Explain which source largely agrees and how this source largely agrees with this middle way
- Explain how the sources agree and disagree with each other regarding this middle way
- Use small quotes
- Use your own knowledge to provide further evidence to support the judgements of this argument
- Use your own knowledge to evaluate this argument

Conclusion

- Explain line of argument logically reconciling differences in historiography
- Form an argument that considers all interpretations covered

Printed in Great Britain
by Amazon.co.uk, Ltd.,
Marston Gate.